WRITE YOUR HEART OUT

Published by Big Shoulders Books
DePaul University
Chicago, Illinois

ISBN: 978-0-692-95921-3
Library of Congress Control Number: 2017956405

Big Shoulders Books logo design by Robert Soltys

WRITE YOUR HEART OUT

CHICAGOLAND TEENS ON RELATIONSHIPS: AN INTERACTIVE ANTHOLOGY

EDITED BY **MICHELE MORANO** AND **BETH CATLETT**
FOREWORD BY **MICHELLE FALKOFF**

ABOUT BIG SHOULDERS BOOKS
Big Shoulders Books aims to produce one book each year that
engages intimately with the Chicago community and, in the process,
gives graduate students in DePaul University's Master of Arts
in Writing and Publishing program hands-on, practical experience
in book publishing. The goal of Big Shoulders Books is to
disseminate, free of charge, quality anthologies of writing by and
about Chicagoans whose voices might not otherwise be shared.
Each year, Big Shoulders Books hopes to make small but meaningful
contributions to discussions of injustice and inequality in
Chicago, as well as to celebrate the tremendous resilience and
creativity found in all areas of the city.

The views and opinions expressed in this book do not necessarily
reflect those of DePaul University or the College of Liberal Arts and
Social Sciences, and should not be considered an endorsement by
DePaul for any purpose.

ABOUT OUR FUNDERS
*Write Your Heart Out—Chicagoland Teens On Relationships:
An Interactive Anthology* was made possible by a grant from the
William & Irene Beck Charitable Trust.

CONTENTS

INTRODUCTION
Michele Morano and Beth Catlett

IN 1969, WHEN FRED ROGERS TESTIFIED before the Senate Committee on Communications in order to preserve funding for public television, he explained that one function of his children's program, *Mr. Rogers' Neighborhood*, was to "make it clear that feelings are mentionable and manageable." Emotions were a central part of each episode, and the show encouraged its audience to pay attention to and discuss them. That, according to Senator John Pastore, was worth the twenty million dollars PBS had requested.

Long after *Mr. Rogers' Neighborhood* went off the air, the importance of talking about and managing emotions remains, for children and adults alike, and particularly for teens who are learning to negotiate the complexities of relationships. Exploring and reflecting on feelings, as well as on the experiences that prompt them, is a radical act that can prompt positive social change. Big Shoulders Books aims to promote social justice by disseminating stories that might not otherwise be told, and we believe paying attention to the messages young people absorb and tell about relationships is an important component of lessening the physical and emotional distress that is too often part of the teen years.

Beth has worked with teens in a number of capacities, including through Take Back the Halls, the fifteen-year old program she began with community partner Heather Flett in response to an epidemic of teen dating violence. Through this work, she has witnessed the incredible capacity of young people to focus with keen insight on the complex dynamics of relationships. Michele, too, has worked with adolescents and teens in many creative writing workshops and been impressed by the perceptiveness and power of young people reflecting on their own personal experience. This book arose out of our desire to hear about how teens negotiate the burdens, delights, disappointments, and *feelings* of love, including romantic love, friendship, and familial love. We are both committed to sharing the stories of an age group that is too often talked about more than listened to.

Our call for submissions for this volume specified creative nonfiction writing in either essay or poem form. As powerful as short stories can be, and as much truth as fiction contains, we want to showcase the messy reality of actual lives. We want readers to feel the energy and vulnerability of the nonfictional narrator that is at once grammatically singular ("I") and contextually plural, a combination of the self who went through an experience and the self writing about it. We want to encourage and celebrate the act of reflection that is necessary for building empathy, compassion, and understanding.

This anthology would not have been possible without the hard work and commitment of classes in DePaul University's MA in Writing and Publishing program, and students in Michele's Book Editing course were instrumental in developing this volume. Both graduate and under-graduate students read and edited submissions, often making suggestions for revision that we shared with the authors. DePaul students also dis-seminated the call for submissions widely, with two students going into local schools to lead creative nonfiction workshops about relationships. Students in the Book Publicity course taught by Dana Kaye prepared a plan for launching the book into the world.

During the editing process, contributors who revised and resubmit-ted their work often included notes of appreciation for the attention paid to their writing and were wonderfully cooperative as we negotiated changes. We were inspired by this back and forth process, and after learn-ing that one high school creative writing club encouraged its members to use the writing prompts contained in our call for submissions to generate ideas for their narratives, we decided to make this anthology interactive. What follows is a collection of works by teen authors interspersed with Invitations to Write and space for readers to capture their own stories and ideas. One such invitation encourages readers to use images, cre-ated by Chicagoland teens in classes at the arts organization Marwen, as a jumping-off point for writing. An additional list of writing prompts appears at the end of the book, along with a list of local organizations that foster teen writing.

Our hope as editors, educators, and social justice advocates is that the creative nonfiction works collected here will prompt readers to contemplate how intensely we humans love and desire, beginning at a young age, and how profoundly the relationships around us influence our own. We believe strongly that Mr. Rogers' goal of bringing feelings into the light remains a worthy one, as is the act of managing those feelings in life and on the page, in well-crafted works of literature that reach out and connect.

FOREWORD
Michelle Falkoff

I HEARD A NEW SONG on the radio a while ago. The lyrics were hard to understand at first, and the structure was simple—verse-chorus-verse-chorus-bridge-chorus, with few chord changes and only the occasional soaring note in the melody (though here I should admit that occasional soaring notes are one of the few things in life that make my eyes water in a way I would definitely not refer to as crying). I didn't think much of the song other than that I liked it okay and that I probably wouldn't change the channel when it came on again.

When it came on again, the lyrics were a bit more comprehensible, and it became clear the song was about someone trying to convince his love that physical distance would not separate them even though he had to go away for a while. After another listen I could hear the singer defending his failure to stay in touch, swearing that he would come home if his love really needed him; I could hear in his voice that he meant it, even as I could understand why his love might find that insufficient. The ache of his insistence, the parallel ache of my understanding that his claims might not be enough—that ache was visceral and familiar.

Then I bought the single on iTunes and listened to it enough to feel chastened that I'd ever thought it was a simplistic song. The melody moved to unexpected places; the soaring notes definitely made the not-crying eye-watering thing happen; and when I tried to work out the chord structure on the piano, it turned out to be far more complex than I'd expected.

So I listened to it about a thousand more times. After hitting repeat for the 1001st time, I noticed my eyes stayed dry during the soaring notes. I could sing along to the lyrics in the car without being aware I was doing it, without hearing the words themselves, without thinking about what they meant. The song was becoming background noise. I stopped putting it on repeat, though I still sang along when it came on the radio.

And then, one day, the song came on the radio and I changed the channel.

Many of the writers in this anthology will recognize the structure of my relationship with this song. It's also the structure of most of my high school romantic relationships, though back then I lacked the insight to see it, much less the talent to express it as powerfully as the writers here have done. The stories and poems in this book brought me to that aching place, where longing was everything and I spent most of my mental energy trying to understand why relationships did or didn't work out, why the sheer force of my desire for some boy in my class—some undiscovered treasure only I could recognize—wasn't enough to make him love me back.

The ache was everything for me, then. It's a hard feeling to remember now, though I can get it back once in a while when I listen to the right song. Or when I read the right book, like this one. Michael Gonzalez's "Looking Back on Love" exemplifies the ache, the pain of feeling like you've found someone who could be right for you and that person doesn't see you the same way. "Love shouldn't be forced on someone," he says, and that statement shows a depth and maturity that should be commonplace, though anyone who reads the news knows it is not. Jazmin Carmona's "Six Long Years" seems to be about the ache, and yet its structure tells us that she's really writing about the best antidote to the ache: friendship.

One of my favorite things about this collection is how writers like Michael and Jazmin eschew traditional romantic narratives to describe their actual experiences and feelings. They evoke the ache perfectly, along with the recognition that, unlike in a lot of fiction, the story doesn't always end the way we want it to. The visceral and familiar feeling I got when listening to that song was everywhere in these pages; I have no doubt that a number of these writers will go on to write the kinds of books I want to read.

And they'll be writing about more than just the ache. Any book that asks for writers to articulate their hearts has to be bigger than that. In this volume are beautiful narratives about those who managed to find love, even if it didn't stay, like Mike Arruela's "Love is Everything," about family relationships, good and bad; like Francesca Lemke's "Flashback,"about complicated friendships that may or may not have the potential for romance; like Maggie Palomo's "I Know." The writers are brave and straightforward in their willingness to tell the truth about the events of their lives, how they felt about those events, and what they learned from them, and that knowledge is substantial and apparent on every page.

The breadth and depth of content in this collection reminds me that if falling for a song is like having a crush, then falling in love for real is more like learning to love the whole album, appreciating the variety of songs and how, different as they may be, they come together to form a unified whole. Really great albums don't get boring after repeated listening; they change and adapt and mutate so that every listening reveals something new. They're complicated and sometimes contradictory and sometimes flawed and always real and they're better than any one individual song, even if each song can be a favorite at one time or another. This book has become one of my favorite albums, and I hope it will become one of yours as well.

A CLEAR KISS
Estefania Martinez Limo

———— ≫♥→ ————

I STILL REMEMBER THE FEELING of that rainy afternoon when my eyes met someone else's. My first love, my first crush. I had never felt like this before, like my heart did not belong to me.

This was in my homeland: Chiclayo, Peru. I was six years old and it was toward the end of first grade. My father had died from a heart attack, so we had to move to my grandparents' house, a blue painted-brick house that had three stories and a courtyard. There were many family members living there and also some of the servants. The servants did everything, so I never did chores like other kids. The new school bus I took was white and very little.

On the first day of taking that bus, I woke up at 11 a.m. because I was in the afternoon class and school started at noon. I felt very excited and nervous about boarding the new school bus. It had rained all morning, and I hoped it would not rain in the afternoon. As I was getting ready for school, I imagined the type of people I would meet on the bus. I wondered if there were mean girls and nerdy kids and imagined what group I'd belong to.

When I got on the bus, I did not notice who was there and only looked for a seat. I did not want to see the other kids' faces. I could feel their cold eyes on me and tried to sit close to the window. Then, minutes later, I had a sensation to turn my head. I turned to my right and at that moment could hear my heart beating very fast, and my hands felt very sweaty. That was the moment when love entered my life.

The sun was beaming, and I saw his light brown eyes shining in the sun. He gave off a light like a star. I could not stop staring at him. He appeared to be my *príncipe azul,* my "blue prince." I could hear butterflies flying all around me, but I did not know what the feeling really was at the time. As I was getting off the bus, I still had my eyes on him.

I didn't learn his name that day, but on the second day, the boy and I talked for a bit. I was very shy and quiet. I could see he was trying to get me out of my safety zone, but every moment I was thinking about my dad, down to the tiniest details. Grief surrounded me like a storm cloud. I could see the little boy wanted me to be happy. It was hard for me to smile that first year, but my little crush made me smile for no reason, daydream relentlessly, and feel extra motivated to go to school. My *príncipe azul* helped me not go into complete darkness.

In the second year of school, we talked more and told each other jokes. He always told me cheesy jokes like, "Pepito, tell me four members of the cat family: Father Cat, Mother Cat and two kittens." At recess, we played more games and ate together. I was in class A and he was in class C. Even though we had different classes, he became a dear friend to me. We played around on the bus and he teased me. He hit me on my shoulders and I responded in kind. The school driver always told us to sit down because we were running around. Then the people on the bus started telling us that we were in love. They said that between love and hate there is only one step and that we were on it. I did not understand what they were talking about, so I just kept playing.

One normal day after school I was getting off the bus when I felt a sticky thing on my mouth. It was a piece of clear tape that a girl put against my lips, and then I felt the pain flow away. In slow motion, I saw her put the same piece of clear tape to his lips. I could not believe they had just done that. I didn't know what to do, so I just got off the bus and walked the rest of the way home. That image of him with the tape on his lips was on my mind all night. I wondered if that tape was a kiss or not and what I should do the next day.

In the morning I didn't know how to act. I thought he would be mad at me, and I felt ashamed. On the bus, I tried to avoid his eye and every time our eyes met, I quickly looked down. When we got to school, I was the last one to get off the bus. I was close to getting to the school door when I felt a warm grasp. I turned and saw him. I was too nervous to see his eyes, and I did not want to talk about what had happened. In that second, I thought he did not want to be my friend or maybe he wanted to tell me to forget everything that had happened. I lifted my face and our eyes met. Within seconds I felt a soft touch on my lips, and then he ran away. I stood there in shock. That kiss got through to my soul. I'd had my first kiss with my first crush, my first love. It was like a story out of a fairy tale.

Now my love stories are not as innocent and full of thrills as that first one. But I remember the moment when my taped kiss touched his lips and wonder if he ever thinks of me or if I am just a lost memory of childhood.

THE FORGOTTEN
Terey Tellez

WE WERE BEST FRIENDS. We'd built that reliance, that connection, that bond. We played games together in your room and acted like we couldn't hear your parents fighting in the living room. We would play Yu-Gi-Oh! like we couldn't hear the pounding or your sister crying. We would eat together, rush to finish before the head of the household, the provider, began yelling and scolding about anything that was an inconvenience. We would play with your cousins in the backyard when those guests were over to visit your father's business in the house. Then, before I realized it, I would be the one inviting you over to my house. But when I moved away, involuntarily, we couldn't say goodbye. I visited once or maybe twice before two years into high school, and saw you did the same things we used to do, but with a different friend.

Now we've gotten in contact again after all the years, and I don't really recognize you. Your family has split, like the spirit from flesh. You mimic your father who has dispersed the family, your voice hoarse. I've stopped trying to get together, concluding there isn't much left between us. I can continue to remember the good times we had and tell myself that we can make more in the future, but I know we were just a chapter in each other's lives. One that ended in an inconclusive sentence, with an epilogue that foreshadowed another chapter that'll never come.

I'll miss you, my dear friend. I hope you will be happy and content one day. I hope you'll realize that the drugs, the friends who are lost themselves, and the women without respect mean nothing but temporary pleasure. They can't fill in a void left by what you went through. A part of me also hopes that I can be there when you realize this, so I can comfort you again.

WHO NEEDS ENEMIES?
Preethika Somarapu

———————⟫—♥—→———————

ON THE FIRST DAY of third grade, I stomped around the playground, still pretty miffed about the whole moving schools fiasco. Who wouldn't be a little annoyed at having to leave all of your friends and people you know to go a school full of strangers? "Well, not totally full of strangers," a little voice in my head said. "There is one person you know."

"No," I argued with myself. "She's a stuck-up know-it-all, and just because Mom and Dad say she's not so bad now doesn't mean it's true."

The "she" I was arguing with myself about was my childhood rival Megha, the bossiest person I'd known. I prided myself on the fact that even though we lived a few streets away from each other, I had managed not to interact with her in about two years.

I was walking laps around the field, the only exercise I have ever willingly done, when I noticed a tall girl on a bench with a few books. She was reading, glaring at the page like it owed her money. I walked over and, being the avid reader I am, said, "Hi, I'm Preethika. Is that book you're reading any good?"

"Hey," she replied. "Yeah, it is. And I know who you are."

Huh? I thought before realizing with a start that she was Megha. I wanted to escape the situation but couldn't and ended up sitting on the bench next to her. "So, um, how was CLA?" I asked, referring to the school where I'd gone for preschool and kindergarten and where our epic rivalry began.

"Good, especially after you left," she said, eyes narrowed, "Don't think I forgot what you did."

What I did? I thought about our early years together and came up with nothing. "What are you talking about?"

"I'm talking about how you told my mom about how I wouldn't let you be the stupid Rainbow Fairy when we were playing."

I vaguely remembered what she was talking about. "I'm sorry that I told on you, but I probably had a good reason like maybe, I don't know, someone was bossing everyone around and I was sick and tired of it."

"That doesn't give you the right to tell my mom!"

"That gives me every right!"

By then I had realized that we were two crazy people arguing on a bench, so I lowered my volume so people passing by wouldn't stare. I turned towards Megha on the bench. "Okay, so now that we've established that we're both crazy and like books, shall we be friends?" I questioned.

She scrunched up her nose. "Huh?"

"I mean, it makes sense. We're both new here and we know each other pretty well, so why not?"

Megha smiled. "If you're not going to stab me in the back the second my eyes are turned, then sure. Why not?"

We shook on it, and little did I know then but the former bane of my existence would become my best friend. Just don't tell her, or she'll hold it over me forever.

PAPER MEMORIES
Miranda Sun

⟶♥⟶

i.

IT'S FEBRUARY, and winter is still in full force. Just last week, Meadow's Edge Elementary had two days off because of cold weather, which was great because I was sick and didn't want to miss school. Now I'm back to hoping something will happen in two days. Valentine's Day telegrams are still being delivered, although I haven't gotten one yet.

Still, I don't expect it when *he* walks up to me and asks if I've gotten his telegram.

My eyes widen. No, I haven't!

He tells me he'll try to find it, smiles, and walks away. My heart dances in anticipation. He's sending me a telegram! That *must* mean something, right?

After school, my dad gives my sister and me fortune cookies. I break out the paper fortune and carefully set the two halves of my cookie on my plate, brushing pale golden crumbs off my fingers. I've heard that if you eat your cookie before you read your fortune, it won't come true.

I unfold the slip of paper, hoping that it's a good one. It says: *There will be a happy romance for you shortly.*

What if it means what I think it means? I reread it again, turning the words over in my mind. Luckily, neither my dad nor my sister ask me what I got, and I put my fortune near my plate before picking up the cookie. It's crunchy and sweet and tastes perfect.

I write about the day in my diary. At the bottom of the page after the P.P.S. where I write about what he said to me, I draw a heart with an arrow through it.

ii.

It's a Friday in early March. The bell has just rung, and I'm walking toward the front doors like everyone else, backpack straps firmly on my shoulders. The air is full of voices from the kids streaming through the wide lobby. I've taken this path a thousand times. The brick-red tiles under my feet and the red brick walls around me are still the same. But today, something is different.

Today, he and one of his friends come up to me. He says, "I heard you liked me. Do you?"

Fear strikes in my stomach like a spear piercing the belly of a fish, caught in the previous safety of a school. What can I do? I have to say something.

"Yes," I whisper, and then I flee. I don't know what's going to happen. I have the whole weekend to try to forget.

On Monday, he comes up behind me in line.

"Hey," he says. I barely looked at him in class today.

I turn my head toward him but don't look him in the eye.

"I like you too," he says. "You're nice."

This time I lift my gaze, startled but hopeful. Our eyes meet. He smiles.

iii.

It's late March. The school day is almost over at Meadow's Edge Elementary. Students are packing up, stuffing their colorful folders and pencil cases into their backpacks. A few impatient ones are already standing by the door, scuffing their shoes on the speckled gray and brown carpet. The teacher herds them away from the hallway, reminding them that they must wait until the bell.

I'm still at my desk putting my homework into my folder, trying not to crease it. I put my pencils into their box and slide it into my backpack. Anticipation wiggles inside me, caterpillars who are not yet old enough to be butterflies. I lift my eyes and search the room.

There. He's just joined the back of the flock of kids waiting to leave. I open my homework folder again and slide out a set of origami pencils, taking care not to crinkle them. I smooth out any creases. I want him to like my gift, and crinkles are not in the plan. When we had our Valentine's Day class party, he asked me for a red crane, so I know he definitely likes origami. After brushing my thumb once more over the fragile surface of the royal blue colored pencil, I get up, pulling the straps of my backpack firmly over my shoulders.

I quicken my pace, slipping in after him just as he turns his head.

"Hi," I say, my voice quiet amongst the chatter of milling kids.

"Hi," he answers, smiling.

"Today's your birthday, and I know you like to color, so I, um, thought you might like these. I made them myself yesterday." I hold out the colored pencils.

He looks surprised but smiles. "Thanks."

I duck my head shyly. What do I do now? Thankfully, the bell rings, and his friend yells at him to come on. I walk out of school at my own pace, smiling.

iv.

I move away.

I never see him again.

I don't like moving. It means I have to leave behind the friends I have and make new ones, get used to a new bedroom and a new classroom. And nothing can prepare you for it.

But in time, I forget what it feels like as I build a new life in a new town—at least, until it's time to tear it down and set off again.

v.

Years later, this memory is still relatively intact. I am the sort of person who carefully tucks ticket stubs into her purse and then leaves them littered around the floor, the sort of person who arranges objects to line up just so on her bookshelves and then leaves them to collect dust, the sort of person who makes friendships and then leaves them behind, or is left behind herself. My memories are divided by moves—from Missouri to Florida to Indiana to Iowa to Illinois. I am the sort of person who still imagines meeting up with people she used to know, yet has no real plans to make it happen.

My life is not a book, but a stack of papers. A messy, haphazard pile composed of torn-out notebook paper, old birthday invitations, thank-you notes, and forgotten paper fortunes. They can be reordered and written upon and amended, and they can fall.

The first time I tried to remember what happened with the elementary school boy, I remembered falsely, and it became another story, tinted and reordered by the timid insecurities of the self I am today. I read the diaries I kept when I was younger to put truer events on the page. And although seven-year-old me was much more open and therefore braver, she still kept secrets, even from her future self.

Now I wonder. From the process of remembering, I have found out just how much the brain fills in the blanks when confronted with the need to make sense of the dust-covered records in its attic. It connects dots, underlines days it thinks were significant, and, with a curve of the pencil, turns an uncertain set of the mouth into a satisfactory smile.

So how much does *he* remember?

Does he recall a girl with a pink rose in her ink-black hair? Does he wonder where she went? Has he cleaned out his room, found a set of faded origami colored pencils, and thought, *Where did these come from?*

WHO MADE A BIG IMPRESSION *on you early in your life? What former friend or early love do you still think about? Write about an interaction with that person using as many specific details as you can recall.*

Although you're writing about the past, try using the present tense as Miranda Sun does in "Paper Memories."

GENUINE
Kara Kowalski

THE BAR STOOL IS STURDY underneath me as I sit and watch my mom and grandma clean up the kitchen. My grandma insists that she's fine, as she runs the maroon plates underneath the streaming faucet, but my mom encourages her to sit down and visit.

"Seriously, Mom, just sit down and talk with us. It's our last night here," my mom says.

"Oh please, I am perfectly capable of doing both," she responds stubbornly.

"Then at least let me help you," my mom insists. My grandma finally accepts and they begin to work side by side at the sink, while I sit on the stool talking with them.

Our conversation shifts to my sister, who is currently living in Norway with her boyfriend, finishing her master's degree in early childhood education.

"Mom, I miss Jor so much. I can't wait until she comes home for Christmas," I say. Although I was just with her a couple of weeks ago, when I had the opportunity to visit her by myself in Norway, I miss her incredibly. Honestly, I think that because my time with her is limited since she lives in another country, the memories I have of us are all the more special. I have a great appreciation for the time I get to spend with her, and I can't help constantly wishing I was with her.

I think about my time in Norway and flash back to her arms around me as she comforted me on her apartment balcony. She told me everything was okay while the sharp, cool air whipped around us. At the time I wanted to go home, but I knew I would miss her so much. There is no doubt in my mind that she is where she needs to be, and I'm ecstatic for her, but that doesn't mean I don't wish she was closer to home. She inspires me and in a lot of ways shows me what love should be like.

When I was visiting, I remember putting on my boots and heading to the door with her right behind me. I paused and looked at myself in the mirror before walking out of the cozy apartment. Her boyfriend followed us to the door and said goodbye. I continued down the hall after responding, my boots squishing down the blue carpet of the hallway as I walked toward the elevator. Before I got there, I turned and caught my sister waiting for a kiss by the door. Her boyfriend's eyes glanced my way and he said, "Jor, Kara's here." I awkwardly turned around, averting my eyes, but I saw him kiss her sweetly. Then she happily followed me to the elevator.

Although simple, it was one of the most tender moments I have ever seen and makes me think about the love I hope to find in my life. The reason this moment made such an impression on me is because I felt the authenticity of their relationship and understood that my high school relationships just barely scratched the surface of what Jor and her boyfriend had. I knew that high school relationships do not have the greatest track record for lasting very long, but when you are in them it's exciting and exhilarating. For the first time you get to experience what you think love is. As a teenager, my view of love is pretty strictly confined to romantic comedies, which I adore. The very real moment between my sister and her boyfriend influenced me and revealed to me that love is made up of the little moments shared between people. I see love between my sister and her boyfriend when they kiss goodnight, when they make dinner together, when one of them offers to make a trip to the store, and in the countless other small instances of consideration.

I can still picture them working side by side in their small kitchen while I sit at the table cutting vegetables and controlling the music that fills the room. That image of two people as equals, working together, is what love is, and that is what my sister showed me.

Although I miss her, I can't help focusing on how happy my sister is, how she lights up with her childlike optimism that wills everyone close to her to smile. I think that if I didn't know she was happy and with someone who cares about her so much, it would have been impossible for me to leave her, even for a short time. During my time in Norway, she showed me not only what romantic love should be like but also the unconditional love between sisters.

With her on my mind, I wander over to my mom's computer. The screen lights up and I quickly move the curser to iPhoto. After a few minutes of searching I find what I am looking for, a picture of my sister and me with our arms intertwined and smiles on our faces. I then transfer the photo to my phone with satisfaction. It comforts me to have that picture so close, even if she isn't.

MY BROTHER'S KEEPER
Sam Blanc

⟫⟶♥⟶

I OFTEN FELT STRANDED at family gatherings, a sprout of a human in a forest of adults trying their hardest to figure out just how much of a person I was so far. These were the kinds of interactions that led to inquiries about my love life at age seven, yet shock that I could read at age ten.

My brother was the only thing saving my sanity. Of course, I wasn't supposed to talk to him during these events. I was supposed to make polite eye contact and tilt my head inquisitively as my aunts told me that I needed to go to temple more, and that hemp kills cancer, and that the government was trying to take away our guns. My brother and I whispered anyway. We'd laugh about how the soup my aunt spent four days on both looked and tasted like dishwater, and how my uncle's nose bore a distinct resemblance to that of Nigel Thornberry.

We were the outsiders at these events, my brother especially. He looked remarkably different from the rest of my family. My mom's hair is dark brown, almost black, while my dad's hair, or what's left of it, sits atop his head, a meager clump of chestnut wisps. I'm somewhere in the middle, with medium brown hair that contorts around my face like it's trying to escape, no matter how much product I use to weigh it down. Mason's hair was bright yellow: a sunflower, lemon, rubber duck kind of yellow. Not that I cared. Not that I really even noticed. To me, Mason was a partner in adventure, not the odd man out in a monochromatic Christmas card aesthetic.

There was one more thing that made Mason a little different from the rest of us: he didn't actually exist.

As an only child, alone in my creaky, old house for more hours than I'd care to admit, I made myself an imaginary little brother. I have a lot of imagination, at least I like to think I do, so Mason was not my only creation. When I was little, I was a professional dog trainer with an adorable, impeccably trained, mind-reading Yorkie who was fierce despite his minuscule size. Then I was a super spy in a secret underground organization. Then I was half-kid, half-bat: a badass mutant 12-year-old running away from my mad scientist captors in order to avoid being used as a weapon for nefarious purposes. Even as my imaginary scenarios got more realistic, based heavily on the crime, violence, and tragedy I saw on TV, my imaginary worlds never involved the real me. My suspension of disbelief covered half-bat mutants and highly-trained, secret agent tweens, but not the fact that boring little me could be involved in any of this cool stuff.

That's what made Mason different. He was the only figment of my imagination that was there with me in the real world. He wasn't a character separated by the limits of reality; he was a human kid, just like me, imagined in a world where he could really exist.

In third grade, I had a real-life friend named Olivia. She was the kind of kid that hid tyranny under a reverberating laugh and a wide smile. She said swear words. I thought she was absolutely the coolest.

It was crazy how different I could feel at school when Olivia was around. I went from being a kid who sat in the attic talking to an imaginary, yellow-haired boy that didn't exist, to the coolest kid in school—or so I thought. Olivia would say things like, "Reading is stupid" and "Grownups can't control me," and I would say, "Yeah!" Of course, I wasn't capable of much intellectual discussion at age eight, but I felt indomitable, and there was something exhilarating about being part of a dynamic duo. I couldn't help but follow Olivia around. She was so certain, so direct and determined and driven, it made me feel like I wasn't just some kid anymore; third grade had a purpose. I had no idea what that purpose was, but I said, "Yeah," again and again, and every time I felt a little bit more important.

I thought I'd found the closest thing to Mason—same yellow hair and blue eyes and even better, Olivia was real. Naturally, real friendship presented some challenges. For one, I had to make sure she liked me. Mason was me, so we pretty much agreed on everything unless I decided he contradicted me for a convivial argument. Olivia, however, had her own real opinions and I made sure to respect them and take them to heart—and to not challenge them.

No one really messed with us. This was partially because as a baby, Olivia had been badly burned in a fire, so pieces of skin on her arms and legs were folded in on themselves, covered with a shine like a thin layer of plastic wrap. She didn't hide it, though; it was like a shield of pity for the times she talked back, or didn't do her homework, or lied to her parents.

Olivia said some hurtful stuff to me, but I thought she was being brave and honest. As potentially the most unassertive person to ever exist, I respected her candor. So when she told me I should never wear my hair down because it looked like a rat's nest, or that I was weird for "like-liking" a boy with glasses, I just said, "Yeah," and went along. I thought of her as like Mason because siblings are always poking fun at each other. Soon I found out that there was something a little more nefarious to her taunting.

I used to be excited to walk to my classes alone: no teacher, not confined to a single-file line, but it got old after the first week of school. Independence was overrated. I was thinking about that when I saw Sophie running down the hallway to talk to me. She came to tell me that Olivia was mocking me in computer class.

Apparently Olivia said I was weird because I would sometimes hum quietly to myself during class. Looking back, that is probably the most pathetic insult I've ever heard. I mean, if the best someone can do to mock you is say that you hum at inopportune times, then kudos to you. But I took it pretty hard. I thought she was my friend.

I tried not to cry, not to talk about it at all for that matter. I wanted to, but the only thing I was more afraid of than bullying was confrontation. Even now, I do my best to avoid talking to anyone about anything serious. So I didn't talk to Olivia, or Sophie, or my teachers, or even my mom or dad.

Later that day, I told Mason about it. I've always been one for self-reflection, but sometimes it's easier to at least pretend someone's there, just so you don't feel like a total idiot when you mumble something out loud.

My nose stayed pointed at the ceiling so that I could almost see him out of the corner of my eye. The light that shone through the crack in the door threw shadows along my pale yellow wall like highlights in tousled blond hair; the iridescent blue light from my alarm clock on my desk imitated the shifting gleam of attentive eyes.

Of course I knew Mason wasn't really there, but when I was talking, some part of my brain went numb, turned a blind eye to reality. Mason didn't say too much in response—he never did—but when he did speak, it was in exclamations.

"That's not okay!"

"You never did anything to her!"

"Some friend she is!"

"At least your humming was on pitch!"

Mason was me, obviously. But it didn't feel like it. He said all the things I didn't feel justified in saying. Hearing Mason's words echo in my head, even if they were just my words at a higher pitch, smooth and sturdy and confident, gave me faith that my thoughts weren't just conjecture spawned from self-pity.

I'd hung out with Olivia because she was loud, but that's all it was: noise. I still aspire to have the kind of confidence she had, and the kind I created in Mason, and I still look for it in other people, although I prefer people who are loud for a reason. At age seventeen, I can't really justify hanging out with a figment of my imagination anymore, but a lot of my friends have the same sarcastic, mocking sense of humor I created in him. I think no matter how old I get, I'm going to wish I had a sibling, and that wish is always going to bring back Mason, hanging out in the back of my mind. I can picture him just as clearly now as when I was eight, rolling his eyes at the kids that talk and manipulate others like Olivia did in third grade.

So he wasn't real. He wasn't physically squished between me and my slobbering dog in our Christmas card. But to me he was family: saying cheese, posing in his Santa hat from the depths of my subconscious mind.

FLASHBACK
Francesca Lemke

***FLASHBACK* TO WAKING UP** to arms enfolding me in a warm, snuggly embrace. I can still smell the vanilla emanating from her hair and feel her bosomy warmth against my cheek. When my mom was away at work in the middle of the night, I sometimes awoke with a startling fear that spread, bit by bit, taking over every part of my being like the tendrils of ivy climbing its way, brick by brick, over our neighbor's house, until no space had been left untouched. This same, creeping feeling left me gasping, sucking in with all my strength. I needed a familiar face and a feathery touch to reassure me that my mom would be back. As each moment ticked by and I looked at the shadows cast on my bedroom wall, I would settle back down into the comfort of my smiling Gram. She always came at the moment I needed her most. She could sense my terror and would quietly be there for me with her encompassing tenderness. Ah, these early memories are always within me in every corner of my mind, in every place.

Flashback to my mom and my dad no longer together. Those were turbulent times, of bickering feuds, half-smiles and half-truths, all thrown together in a blender of make-believe. Listening through the closed door, I grabbed my blanket to wrap around me, cloaking me in its material warmth and mesmerizing me with its intricate, swirling patterns that lulled me into a sense of calm, false that it might have been. More fear and confusion washed away the once safe life. Then she suddenly approached, my Gram, to swathe me in her own soft words.

Flashback to a new home and mom's new boyfriend. Tiptoeing around so as not to draw attention to the fiery temperament yet cold disposition of The Beast was a maneuver in itself. Even though I knew deep down in my heart that the turbulence around me was not right, I was too young to voice my fears. No food in the fridge, not because of money problems, but because of the selfish whims of a depraved lunatic who wanted to have a pencil-thin wisp of a woman. Oh, how I longed to sink my teeth into two all-beef patties, special sauce, lettuce, cheese, pickles, onions on a sesame seed bun. Instead, I hid packages of bologna under my bed and snuck potato chips and granola bars into my dresser drawers. I sure wasn't a poster child for hunger, but the times that I was able to leave the lair on non-school days were a relief. There was never a hand laid on me, but sometimes emotional and mental anguish can be even worse than physical pain. My mom did the best she could under those restrictive circumstances; however, it was Gram's love and support that helped me to mend.

Flashback to hearing my mom cry. The piercing shriek and then steady wail of inconsolable suffering left me frozen on the bottom steps of the stairway leading to the second-floor bedroom. What could a seven-year-old do at this point, not knowing if He was in the room with her? Me, so young, confused, and wondering why we had to live in this cavernous monstrosity of a place with its pseudo beauty. Sometimes I just wanted to click my heels like Dorothy and find a place that we could call home. My wish came true, but unfortunately at the expense of a broken mother, and I mean that in the literal sense. In one crushing moment, she received a whopping punch that cracked her ribs and sent her catapulting down the staircase. Her anguish was indescribable as she lay in a heap on the floor. The sound of the sirens and the flashing lights dispersing their red brilliance in the darkness outside were our beacons of hope. The truth was laid bare to the world of those who loved us, and with Gram and friends in tow, my mom and I were rescued from the ongoing lie.

Flashback to starting all over with a new place and friends who I found were true. That was the beginning of genuine happiness and contentment, of bonding with my mom, of finding myself, and of being able to open a refrigerator door at home without someone hovering over me. I learned how to ride a bike, felt the floating sensation as my feet left the ground and molded onto the pedals, the wind blowing against my face. Roller skating was my next venture, and I can still remember the sound of the wheels against the wood floor, the other kids laughing, my reaching out and holding onto the sideboards for dear life until magically my feet began to take hold and find the rhythm of the gliding motion. I embraced my newfound freedom. My mom was smiling again and actually putting on a few pounds. This new way of life was a discovery for both of us. The doorway opened and never closed again.

Flashback to another catastrophe. My mom had finally found someone she could love, trust, and confide in, whom she found to be mature, understanding, and most of all, approved by me! Then one day she doubled over in excruciating pain, the kind of pain that knocks the wind out of you and makes you feel like your heart is in your throat and your body has inner knives cutting away at the insides. She was rushed to the emergency room, where after hours of probing and tests, nothing came back conclusive. A very concerned emergency room physician suggested that she make an immediate appointment with an oncologist. More tests, biopsies, and probing, and within a few days, she encountered her worse nightmare yet. She had stage four non-Hodgkin's lymphoma, a type of cancer that attacks the body's immune system. My own insides felt as though they were being split apart. I tried my best to put on a brave front and even convinced myself at some point that everything was all right. The pitfalls and worries I was experiencing were, I'm sure, nothing compared to what my mom was going through, but it felt as if the world was coming to an end. I could not even imagine life without her.

Flashback to those cancer-ridden days of holding up my mom's head. She was weary, tormented, growing sicker with each chemo treatment, yet with a resolve of steel. I lay beside her and held onto her, watching the slow rise and fall of her chest as she tried to find a moment's rest while fighting off the urge to spew over the freshly laundered blanket. We didn't know what to expect. My Gram, my mom's loyal boyfriend, and I tried to find comfort within each other, within the dread.

Flashback to tears pouring out and my body shaking. What seemed to be a never-ending battle for my mom was also wearing me down. One moment she felt better. The next she was hunched over in pain. The tremors of the past had found their way back to me and seemed to constantly run through my body. Fear was growing rampant, yet I fought down the desperation by immersing myself in my schoolwork. I had always been an above-average student, but I was motivated to push myself to even higher levels. Books were my friends, and I found solace in them. I also had some extraordinarily sensitive and understanding friends who helped me during this heartbreaking time. My mom kept fighting and forced herself to go to work, even on some days when she just wanted to crawl in bed and hide beneath the covers. The ups and downs of the chemotherapy, trips to the doctor, biopsies and scans, and the aftermath of her remission have made our tight-knit family even closer. My mom is a strong woman, but the courage she displayed during her moments wracked with pain have set her on a pedestal and made her the best possible role model for me. My mommy, my dearest heart, my best friend is one of the women I aspire to be. Gram is another. Gram has been there for both of us and always has understood my heart's aching.

Flashback to holding hands with a boy. This experience came at a time when I needed it most. He wasn't just some cute, smart, amazingly good-looking boy. He was an incredible friend. He understood the hurt and worry over my mother, and there were things I could say to him that I couldn't say to others. Just the touch of his fingertips entwining themselves around mine made my worries disappear, even if it was just for a while. The gentle sway as he pushed me on the park swing brought out the laughter in me, and I would snap a secret shot of him on my phone when I thought he wasn't looking. We were innocent and remained that way, even though we were prodded about our young relationship by classmates who thought they knew everything about life's intricacies. The memory of that beautiful soul and his shy demeanor, even though it was just a short time ago, brings a smile to my face as I remember how my heart filled with joy.

CLADDAGH RING

Alexandra Huizar

>>—♥—→

I.

I SLIP MY RING into the pocket-sized zip lock bag with the red and black biohazard sign; it makes my stomach muscles contract just to take it off. I give the bag to the indignant nurse and stare down at my limp arms and hands where my ring finger is bare. Tears well up in my eyes like an overweight water balloon. Pop.

The ring depicts two golden hands holding a heart. I never imagined I would take off that ring when I first slid it on five years ago. The hands symbolize friendship, and the heart symbolizes love, of course. Originating from Ireland, it's called the Claddagh ring. If the ring is on the right hand next to the pinky and the heart is pointed outwards, it signifies being single and the woman's heart is open. If the heart is pointed inwards, that means the woman is in a relationship. Left hand, ring finger, and the heart pointed outwards, means the woman's engaged. If the ring is worn on the left hand, ring finger, and the heart is pointed inwards, it suggests the woman's married.

Left hand, ring finger, and heart pointed inwards. Every day, I wear it like that. But I'm not married. I'm not even in a relationship.

I remember the day Abuelita gave me the ring

"I know you lost your other ring." My abuelita shook her head and searched her drawer for something. "But I want you to have this one. I've had it for who knows how long." I inspected the tiny ring. "You hold your own heart, mija." She took in a shaky gulp of air. "Just remember that." Child me, who thought I knew everything, nodded and stood there puzzled.

The nurse trudges out of the room and mutters something as quickly as she came in. I climb back on the hospital bed and wrap my arms around my legs. I only see my hands as everything I struggle to hold back pours out. I feel stupid; it's just a piece of jewelry.

The doctor comes in, interrupting my thoughts; a strong sterile smell hugs his white coat. He takes a deep breath and I look down at my hands again. "Ms…," he says, but my eyes can't meet his. I'm looking at my naked finger.

After the doctor leaves the room I whisper to myself the words my abuelita once told me, "Hold your own heart, mija." Here I am five years later, my mental state breaking down. "Is my dad coming?" I ask my mom. Hope rises in my voice. "I don't know. You know him." She rolls her eyes. Just my left hand starts to shake. I stare up at the ceiling and take a deep breath.

"Hey mija, how are you doing?" My abuela peeks around the curtain. I jump up and throw my hands around her neck. Steamy tears roll down my cheeks. Fresh lemon shampoo drifts from my abuelita. I close my eyes and stay in her embrace. She lets go and looks me in the eye. My heart halts, and I hope she doesn't see the missing piece of gold on my finger.

II.

When my mom and dad were together, clothes were thrown out on the dry grass, yelling and screaming echoed down the halls. My dad's bare hands came down on my mom; she was a barking chihuahua, her body shaking. I was five and my sister barely a few months old. One night, I remember my mom woke me up out of bed and I pretended to be asleep, but how could I be when my sister howled and my mom and dad argued? She made me put on my pink *chanclas*, and we followed my dad into the darkness. Her car crept after him trying to find the truth.

Now, my parents are divorced and both have remarried. But it's déjà vu all over again with my mom and stepdad. All the women in my life have been cheated on and are in abusive relationships. One of my mom's sisters would come home with a black eye and say, "I fell down the stairs." My mom's other sister had a controlling boyfriend. The same thing happened with my dad's sister. Abused and controlled. One had to choose her lover over her kids. Then family friends were cheated on, and they'd go back to their unfaithful boyfriends or husbands.

All of these women, the women who care for me and give me advice, were young and "in love." I just can't comprehend it. Maybe they think that's the love they deserve. But every time I look down at my ring and hear my abuelita's voice telling me to hold my own heart, I know that I can't put my happiness or my feelings in someone else's hands. Especially those of a boy. I'm not a "half." I don't need or want to find my other "half." I'm a whole person by myself. The golden hands on the ring are mine, holding my own heart.

THE LION AND THE WOLF
Madison Hahamy

————— ≫ ♥ → —————

AT 5 FEET 2 INCHES of pure muscle, with a frizzy mane hastily tied with an overstretched black ponytail, my mom is a lion. Through her blinding passion for justice and work as a special education lawyer, my mom roars for those unable to advocate for themselves. My mom is a lion who settles for nothing and is impatient over everything: a savage fighter who respects few and loves fewer.

My dad is a wolf, a misunderstood creature whose dislike of conflict is overshadowed by the fierce need to protect his family. A generally calm and secretly sensitive man, he has stormy moods that make everyone around run for cover. My dad is a wolf who prefers to listen, an aloof observer who does not waste words.

The lion and the wolf, naturally dominant creatures, make for a confusing combination. A constant battle for assertion breeds plenty of meaningless arguments. The lion and the wolf, howling and roaring, can exacerbate bickering into a cacophony of chaos. A stray jacket slung onto the stairs transforms into an argument over which parent works harder for the betterment of my and my brother's lives. For a long time I didn't understood how my parents loved each other, as different as they are. I believed that my brother and I were their sole reason for staying married. And then, I glimpsed their world of subtlety: hurried kisses, movie nights, and last-minute dinner dates. I started paying attention, and realized just how wrong I was.

My first memory of my parents kissing was ten years ago, when we lived in a suburb of Atlanta, in a home atop a hill, surrounded by nature. Before moving to Chicago, my life was different: different school, different friends, different personality. My parents, however, were not. My mom was as fierce as ever, my dad just as strong. It had surprised me, therefore, when I first saw them kiss.

It was after a particularly rough day at work. My dad came home, shoulders slumped as though he were Atlas carrying the weight of the world on his all-too-incapable shoulders. My brother and I were playing, but I had rushed over when I heard the door squeal open just in time to witness their interaction. My mom said nothing, just leaned forwards on the tips of her toes while my dad squatted down at an awkward angle. They kissed each other with the utmost tenderness, a kind of vulnerability that I hadn't known existed. Their lips touched for all of two seconds before they pulled apart, flushed and embarrassed, after noticing me silently standing next to them.

Ten years later, my parents continue to bicker constantly. In their relationship, nothing has changed. But I have. I notice my mom spending extra time cooking lasagna, one of my dad's favorite meals, even though she has a pile of work waiting at her cluttered desk. I notice my dad thanking my mom for dinner every single night, even when she makes meatloaf. I notice my mom laughing so hard at one of my dad's jokes that she must leave the room to compose herself. I notice my dad taking my brother and me out to dinner when my mom is stressed out from work, even though he wants nothing more than to be at home with his family and dogs.

My parents' two-second kiss opened my eyes to what an ideal relationship is. Even though my parents often clash, their love is more romantic than any fairytale.

THINK ABOUT HOW YOUR IDEAS *about relationships have formed. What role models have you had within your family, among friends, in popular culture? How have the relationships you've observed affected the relationships you've been in or would like to have in the future?*

BEHIND THE PERFECT PICTURE

Nathalia Davila

MY MOTHER SAT inches away from me on the couch that held so many bright memories—movie watching, laughter, and our yearly Christmas celebration. Her light blue eyes, filled with tears, were unable to meet mine. The room was silent as I yearned for her to look at me, to validate my premonitions, but, at the same time, I wanted her to let me live in the fantasy that had been my life for eighteen years.

"I know, Mom. I notice the changes."

In that instant, her head shot up and her eyes revealed the intense fear she had been hiding. Looking for the right words to say, she muttered, "What do you mean?"

My brain took a backseat as, without hesitation, I spilled everything I'd been noticing, from the late nights she had spent at the sponsor bar for the girls' softball team to the way she had become hooked on her phone, smiling and anticipating every message. She never used to have time to respond "K" to my messages or be on her phone at all, but now I was getting "I love you" followed by several emoticons.

When I finished speaking, my vision was blurred by tears, but I could not miss the way her eyes got increasingly smaller and veered down. Her tense shoulders relaxed.

Keeping her gaze down, she said, "I met someone. She's on the softball team. I love your father, and I was not looking. I also don't know where this is going to take me, but I need to see it through."

She was relieved to say those words out loud, and I was relieved to hear them. I was happy that she was finally able to be true to herself and live the life she wanted. After all, she had taken me in as her own; she became the mother I had thought I would never have. She deserved the world. But, selfishly, I wanted the situation not to be true, so that I could keep the family unit that I had thought was forever—the one that nurtured me and made me feel safe, even as other aspects of my life drowned me. We sat there hugging, laughing, and crying and didn't talk about the future.

My biological mother had not played a prominent role in my life; occupied with her own agenda, she was gone by the time I was three. My dad, embracing fatherhood, struggled like any single parent.

Luckily, his boss at the time was compassionate and understanding. Confiding in her, he told her about every hurdle he conquered to keep me, as well as all of the sacrifices he made. Looking into his eyes, she saw the immense love he had for his daughter. Her interest in him grew as she admired his strength and persistence. They opened up to each other, sharing past experiences that only a few other people knew. In time, they were seeing each other outside of the workplace.

As the relationship evolved, she found herself taking on the role of my mother. Having lost her own daughter years before, she yearned for her own family and found happiness in being a part of his. On the other end, my dad loved her humor and the way she took the time to care for me: buying me toys, playing with me, and adding a girly touch to my room by painting the walls purple. Fast-forward four years and many dates later, I walked down the aisle throwing flower petals, some even landing in my grandmother's hair.

These were the two people I called mom and dad. They spent their days cracking jokes and always looking for a good laugh. With many of the same interests, they both participated in races together, supporting each other with a little friendly competition every step of the way. On weekdays, they got home from work, and she made dinner as he sat close by to discuss their days.

Then came the weekends full of softball games, in which she played first base and he pitched. They hosted parties together, during which their friends would always say, "You're so great together," or, "Why can't I find someone that complements me the way you guys have each other?"

Throughout these fifteen years of marriage, everyone witnessed the magnetic pull that defined their marriage. What people failed to see was the underlying tension and arguments. Despite the perfect picture, discord crept in like a hazy fog, wrenching my insides and telling me something was off.

An end of a relationship is similar to a death, with the same disbelief, mourning, anger, and acceptance. In the middle of the end, these emotions are magnified.

For hours after our talk, I was in shock. Even after I knew the truth, our living conditions were still very similar. We were all in the same house, and my parents did not cease to bond with one another. It was as though my father became my mother's best friend through this time of uncertainty. They had long talks about life, and my father supported her much like she supported him.

But, like before, not everything was as it seemed. Looking closely, I could see my father hoped that maybe things could go back to the way they were, and, in some ways, I felt the same. Despite this feeling of hope, we knew it was for the best, and I spent every day reminding myself things would work out in the long run. Overall, I believe my father and I were blinded by the surrealism of my mother's newly discovered sexuality, somewhat believing it wasn't true.

What woke me up to the end of their relationship was the love my mother emitted. Yes, she loved my father, but it was love that was similar to having a dream job—one that made you happy, but not one you wanted to continue in your leisure time. Her new love was different; her smiles were accompanied by a radiance that filled the room and were much more frequent than they used to be. The seemingly picture-perfect marriage had revealed its harsh strokes and imperfect lines. It was no longer even a picture once you looked closely. Sometimes, no matter the strength of the connection, the beauty of love, or the investment put forth, relationships change course, and we must follow their path.

LOSING FAITH
Aurora Harkleroad

WALKING HOME from school, I ducked beneath the bridal wreath along the front porch. It was one of the last days before summer, and I was excited to move to my new school in fall. A black shape stumbled quickly across the porch before I could catch its face. My mom was at the front door, clutching the frame. Her black and green hair was tossed in every direction, lips raw, and she was winded.

"Who was that?"

"No one, just a friend!" She giggled, trying to soften my abrasive attitude. I looked out towards the street, but his motorcycle was already winding around the corner.

A low whistle blew through the school hallways, and I searched for its source, swearing it was right here. I turned my head and Viola was lounging on the stairwell. Nobody else was in the halls, so we could play as much hide-and-seek as we wanted.

The days were sun-spattered as we awaited the next performance. The hours passed with flirting and flower painting. This would be the second year I'd had a crush on her, but I was satisfied with being friends for now. She played every instrument beautifully. I was beginning to experiment with the harp, but I stuck to playing the violin for our concerts.

My mom had been going out with friends on the weekends extensively, and now she hadn't come back for an entire day. I started to worry. None of my texts were getting a response, so I started searching for her location on different apps.

My dad sat on the front porch behind the bridal wreath, but all of the flowers were gone. Spring had passed.

"Where is she?" I asked.

"Nowhere important. I know where she is," he grumbled, but then he chuckled. My worry was replaced with an overwhelming curiosity. I called my grandmother, but she didn't have a clue where my mom might be. My brother hadn't even noticed she was gone.

It was 2 a.m., and I was desperately trying to go to sleep. I wanted nothingness. I wanted indifference and patience. I wanted every emotion to be sucked into the void of space and my eyes to be filled with emptiness. The guy on the motorcycle had tried to kill her the night before.

As she walked up the stairs her eyes were wide, emphasized by her gaping mouth. My father's feet sleepily trudged to the bathroom. Our bathroom doesn't have a closeable door, so the harsh yellow light streamed into the hallway, and he stood there, waiting for her to seek his sympathy. She stared blankly at her phone, entranced by the speed of her texting thumbs. I sat in my bedroom, and like my father, waited for something to be said.

It was winter, and I had found the perfect study spot. The shop felt like a huge, decorated basement. A movie was constantly playing in the waiting area, and the chairs were large enough to hold me and all of my schoolwork. My mother worked silently at her desk, waiting for the next phone call.

Even from prison, he insisted on calling every few hours. No, he wasn't in prison for what he had done to her. I do not know where to start with why he was there. My mother waited, trying to construct the truth from fragments of words, not wanting to believe he could be a liar.

I was fortunate to have friends. Clara's family was so perfect. I felt like a rat there. Her parents lounged on the couch together, blissfully embracing one another. Their three children sat beneath them, having a family movie night. I sat on the arm chair across from everyone.

They were untouched by the anguish of abuse. The adversity faced by queer society was foreign or maybe nonexistent to them. Sure, this family had suffered great hardship, but they faced it together. I felt like a gross stain on their fine white carpet. I knew I couldn't stay there forever.

It was another hard night, with thoughts pounding through my head. When I first fell in love, it wasn't instant. Viola had always been first and foremost my friend. It took months before I grew a crush on her, and years to fall in love. She was my friend, and the first person who hadn't irritated me once. Not a single time.

I couldn't tell anymore if all of this was a coping mechanism. I still can't tell if what I felt was love or just true and absolute friendship that I somehow misunderstood as romantic love. I mean, who doesn't want their lover to also be their best friend?

The moon had passed by this point and my dad walked in from a night at work. He didn't know I was awake. He lit himself a cigarette, washed his feet in the bathtub, and placed a bottle of Jack Daniel's next to him. The odd part was that he was blasting reggae and sitting solemnly in the yellow bathroom light. He'd never even liked reggae, at least according to my mom.

I was going on a trip with the girl I was in love with. I couldn't begin to process this. I felt wrong going across the world with someone who I held unrequited love for. She was my friend, and that was how we would be together. I told myself I had to stop these feelings. Soon.

"I don't love your father anymore because he's never done what I've asked him. The house has been a wreck for years, and he's never done anything to fix it." We were sitting in the car, and my mom was furious over the broken front porch.

She continued to rant. I felt worn out from her talking about every irritating thing my father did. The man she was with wouldn't solve any of these problems either, so I knew that she was only saying these things out of spite.

"Isn't he just as much of a slob? He doesn't even have a job. Where he lives is not even habitable, so what could he do for any of your problems with Dad? Does Dad deserve this?"

"Well, at least he takes care of himself. I'm waiting for your dad to do something. Is he just gonna sit there and let some other man ruin his life? Is he gonna let some other man make him want to kill himself?" Black tar was sticking to every word, poisoning my ears.

"But what if he does kill himself?"

"I guess he irritates me so much I just want him to die sometimes."

I sat down next to my father and fell asleep as he scrolled through his phone. My dreams were filled with a feeling of betrayal stronger than anything I had ever felt. Everything, from the sidewalk around our house to the streetlight was drenched in a sense of betrayal. Images of her boyfriend flickered past my eyes: his excessive brutishness, his vanity.

My entire body tensed up and for the first time, I genuinely wanted to kill someone. I woke up weeping, feeling as if the world had damned me. And I realized that must be how my father felt.

Viola's mom went out to the grocery store, so music was bursting throughout the room. I was looking at Viola upside down on the bed. Suddenly the music stopped, and a moment of concentrated silence passed. Our eyes locked without reason. Our faces were so close and I wanted to kiss her so badly. It felt like eons had passed before I finally got up and grabbed a Jell-O packet. *She's straight, she's straight* I reminded myself over and over.

I knew that she was only overly affectionate with me because she pitied me. I didn't want a relationship built on licking each other's wounds with the false hope that being together would fix them.

A cold was passing through our group. Viola was sick, and I was starting to show signs. But we pushed onward. We entered Yonghegong Temple through a path of willow trees. We had free range to go where we wanted, and Viola sat down on some steps and rested while I looked around.

After some time, we reached the final building. I walked in by myself and was suddenly overwhelmed by the largest Buddha statue I had ever seen. It was made from a single tree and was staring benevolently into the distance. Suddenly, I felt Viola's hand entwine with mine. For a long time, we stood there holding hands, staring into what felt like the void.

I rested my head on her lap, silently weeping as the colorful, neon signs of Beijing passed. Her fingers running through my hair were comforting. She knew I dreaded going home. My other friend was moving away, and I had no more houses to crash. For the moment, I found comfort in the 6,000 miles between me and my house.

It was the third time he had tried choking her to death. She had called a hotline for help, but I knew this wasn't the last time she would break up with him. It hadn't been the last time every other weekend they broke up, so why would it be this one?

My grandmother still had faith. "I think this will be the last time. I believe in my daughter." Her face was serene as she knitted some scarves to donate. I remained silent. My father shook his head and chuckled. He knew it wasn't the last time.

Viola had a crush on Frank. This was degrading. I couldn't remain in love with someone who would never love me back. I'd lost so much of myself to her, and this only meant I had to take back my autonomy. *My mind, my personality, and my ability will not be measured by how much it appeals to her* kept running through my head as I paced around my room.

My room was so small, but it had enough space to let me walk back and forth plenty of times.

I awoke to a thundering series of knocks at the front door. It shook the front side of the house.

"I'm gonna put your husband in the *fuckin'* hospital!" he roared from outside. The dog barked in response. I clamped my hand around his muzzle. "Please shut up Max," I pleaded with him quietly. My mom went outside to deal with him. I tried to crack the window open to hear what was happening, but I only caught indecipherable fragments. He finally left with a brutish gait.

My dad sat on the top of the stairs watching, shotgun in one hand and a cigarette in the other. He saw me staring, and his grey eyes softened.

"I just want you to know, this isn't how relationships are supposed to be."

Here I am now, in the same room where I forced myself to fall out of love with Viola. I think back to all of the times I loved her, and how happy I was then. Waltz music echoes off of the walls, the same music I imagined we would dance to.

I have nowhere I feel truly comfortable anymore. For a moment, I understand my mother.

FOR THE LOVE OF READING

Domino Jones

WE'RE READING *The Scarlet Letter* by Nathaniel Hawthorne in English class right now. It has difficult language, very deep concepts, endless symbols, and requires a lot of reflection in its study. But reading it has felt very different from how my sister described reading her favorite book. A specific chapter I remember reading takes place on a dark, cold October morning and presents the adulterers and their beautiful daughter as they unite in the purifying, truthful light of day. They live through passion and instinct, fearlessly pushing against a strong and angry society.

In contrast, as the sun rises and its powerful rays warm up the glossy city around me, I can't help but think about my greatest fear: my dad and his new girlfriend having a child and casting me aside like he did with his last daughter. This is a cycle where one replaces another in his life, like a wheel of unfulfilling love where he is the center.

But this book makes me think that maybe I am wrong. What if I am angry and blinded and dangerous because I make assumptions with little knowledge of what more there is to life? What if I am keeping myself, because of fear, from a life of reality, truth, beauty, and embracing oneself entirely in both good and bad? While I suffer, the anger and resentment so overpowering it keeps me awake at night and distracted during the day, the only way that I find peace, the only thing that brings me back, is to continue reading.

SISTERHOOD
Madeline Hultquist

IT'S DIFFERENT now that she's gone. Fifteen minutes away might not seem like much, but sometimes it feels as though she has disappeared and may never return.

The house feels empty sometimes. Her blinds don't shut every night. I can no longer hear her plugging her phone charger in, the scratching sounds traveling through the house as she searches for the outlet in the dark. Two out of three kitchen stools sit unused these days, their cushions slowly regaining shape after years of overuse. I don't hear her heavy feet, trampling down the stairs like a baby elephant. Now, the only feet going up the stairs are the even, reasonably quiet footsteps of parents tired after a long day of work.

My first memories of her are little more than fragments.

A gently swaying mobile hangs over a crib that I'm too big for. Grandparents and relatives talk loudly downstairs as we are put to bed early. The room is unfamiliar to sleep in, except I can see her. There, in the twin bed. She fiddles with the mesh nets caging her in so she won't roll out of the bed.

I recall sitting in a sunlit closet. The walls and shelves are all white. There are two pairs of the same shoes, little dark red sandals with straps perforated in the style of brogues. One pair is slightly bigger than the other.

Soft pink slippers, made of supple leather and stretchy elastic evoke another memory. The smell of hairspray and sweat washing over me. A new face, waving me into the mirrored room. Uncertainty and nerves, until she hugs me. All is well, and I shyly shuffle into the class.

We fight over the covers in my next reminiscence. Our beds are matching, one yellow and one pink. On laundry day, we can switch colors. I want to, but she doesn't. Since she's the elder, her word rules. I pout, stuck with the sunny yellow cotton blanket instead of the trendy raspberry one.

The stuffed animals sit in orderly lines, not touching. Each one wears a homemade shirt or cape, bearing an unevenly stitched M. We sit together, drawing on the whiteboard. The lesson is going swimmingly, until we disagree on who gets to teach art. Stuffed animals go flying as a battle takes place in the basement.

"Play the fun CD!" is the constant refrain on the drive home from piano lessons. As the car bumps and jumps on the brick road, we dance in our car seats. Feet banging the chairs, arms stretched out in dramatic dances. We sing about states and dreams and railroad tracks until the laughter overcomes us.

Another car trip drags on endlessly. We play BINGO and that alphabet game where you find a sign that starts with every letter. Finally, the straight highway tapers off to a winding road that swerves among the colorful trees. In the backseat, we sit patiently, too old for boosters. When we approach a turn, she screams "JELLO!" and leans into the turn. I follow suit, and we smush together on one side of the backseat until the next turn, when we throw ourselves to the opposite side. Giggles turn into full belly laughs until my head knocks against the seatbelt buckle, and our parents intervene.

"Tell me when you meet Dumbledore," she instructs, handing me the first *Harry Potter* book. I retreat to my bedroom, ecstatic about finally reading the series she recently started. Ten minutes later, Dumbledore appears on Privet Drive. I sprint to her room, where she brushes her teeth next to the hot pink towels hang-drying. After a quick debriefing on the new character, I am sent back to my room to continue reading.

She gets a cell phone first. It's this delightfully pink Nokia flip phone. She can play trial versions of Tetris and Snake on it. She benevolently allows me to try it out for approximately one minute before snatching it back.

I'm in fifth grade, and she's in sixth. We wave excitedly whenever we see each other in the hallways, which confuses my friend. She informs me that she and her siblings would never make intentional contact in public.

Eighth grade stretches out forever, with time seeming to slow down every day. She gets to spend her days in new challenging classes in high school, making new friends and not having a dress code. I'm left behind with the same old people and the same old classes.

Junior year finds us walking to and from school together, chatting about everything and nothing at the same time. Occasionally, when her orchestra lets out early, she finds me during my lunch period. After receiving bad grades, we can vent to each other while walking to Goldilocks.

Goldilocks is the car she used to drive to school. Well, either Goldilocks or The Rust Bucket, depending on how the car behaved. She always drove, and I turned on the seat warmers. A huge country music fan, she always had the radio tuned to 99.5 or 95.5. On the drive home, we would blast the latest hits, singing at the top of our lungs until we got hoarse.

Senior year, I walk to school by myself, and I walk home alone. She's not at the island eating pizza bagels, ready to help me with my math homework. I never blast country music when I'm driving alone.

She used to make the most perfect chocolate chip cookies. Whenever anyone tried to steal cookie dough without asking her, she got extremely territorial. But she gave me the mixer's paddle every time without fail, which was coated with dough and chocolate.

We used to spend the summer lying on the beach and falling down on rollerblades. We precariously rode our bright yellow tandem bike, waving to the little kids who stared in wonder at the bicycle built for two.

Now, she lives in a new room, with a new friend. Our stuffed animals live in the basement, left to teach themselves. Pink Nokias have transformed into sleek iPhones. Sharing every detail of our day has been replaced with a quick weekly recap over FaceTime. I struggle to make cookies that taste as good as hers did. On her bed at home, her favorite stuffed dog sits, left to collect dust.

While our toys have been abandoned, the memories of growing up together are immortalized in pictures, videos, and thoughts. These photos hang on her new dorm room wall and in my bedroom at home.

Until this year, my entire life had been spent with her. I hadn't known what it was like to live without a sister next to me, ready to protect me, laugh with me, and cry with me. When I was born, she was just learning how to walk.

THE MOST IMPORTANT LOVE

Patricia Carteno

I GREW UP in an environment in which affection wasn't shown so frequently. As I started getting older, I wanted to experience love at first sight like all my friends did. I always had little crushes and ended up getting heartbroken. As kids, we all want to feel the little butterflies in our stomach and our heart skip a beat, but man, after a while that fairytale gets so overplayed.

By the time sixth grade ended and I transitioned to seventh, I had grown super insecure. I just wanted to find someone to show and receive love from. What love meant to me then was unhealthy. I met someone who I felt I could be with and love—let's call him Sam. He was very kind and knew how to play with my emotions well. Around this time I hated myself for who I was and how I looked physically. Although he showed me that he so-called cared, Sam would call me by names that, to this day, when I remember them I feel weak and broken and want to shut myself in a room.

Even though Sam hurt me, I missed him. I always felt at fault. And that's the thing about love. We don't realize the damage and suffering we put ourselves through until it's too late. After all this, I knew I wasn't ready for a commitment or anything really. It's too soon for that.

Now I'm a freshman in high school and see all the growth I've done so far. I'm extremely proud of myself. I held my own and learned to love myself for who I was. That's the most important type of love: self-love.

LOVE
Kara Kowalski

Is hot liquid metal,
dry, warm flesh, the
sweet aroma of old
paper stacked high.
It's worn bed sheets,
the tightening of a tie,
brushed and braided
hair.

Love is ripe fruit,
light wind,
ripped jeans.
It's a card played,
a knitted sweater,
an answered phone
call

IN HER POEM *"Love,"* *Kara Kowalski evokes the definition of an abstract concept (love) by using concrete images that can be experienced through the five senses. Write a poem or short piece of prose in which you illustrate an abstraction (love, desire, joy, fear, disappointment, loss, contentment, etc.) through specific sensory images.*

LOVE IS HARD TO FIND
Romero Golden Garcia

FOR ME I GUESS love is a big deal. But it also isn't. See, I always wanted to find the perfect girl to be with so we could be best friends until the end, but whenever I try to take the next step with a girl she tells me one of three things, every time. It's "Sorry, I don't like you that way," which is fine, "But, you're like a brother to me," which is not fine, or, "I thought you were gay," which is definitely not fine.

I've been trying to get a girlfriend since elementary school, and in fifth grade I asked my best friend out and she said exactly this: "Sure." And I was in fifth grade, so I thought that meant, "Yes," and it does ... but not all the time. If you're confused then here is an example: If you ask someone if they can buy you something and they say, "Sure," with an excited or happy look, then that means they have no problem. But if you ask that same question and they say, "Sure," with an annoyed look, then maybe they owe you or something.

So I dated her for a month exactly, and I would show her off to my friends and hug her and walk with her and talk to her and buy her gifts, and guess what? All she wanted to know was if I was willing to go all out on her and by her pricey gifts, and for a fifth grader I think five bucks is a lot just for a fancy pen. By the way, I bought her the pen, and she cheated on me and then told me about the guy she met a while ago in her karate class and how he was really cute. The day she broke up with me, I was crushed. I was pretty good at hiding it, though. I would say to myself, "Heh, probably broke up with me because of my new haircut."

In middle school I dated this one girl and probably shouldn't have. I regret it very much. In seventh grade I had a little crush on her and never did anything about it, so it went away. Then in eighth grade she told me she liked me. Hoping my feelings for her would return, I said, "Yes" when she asked me out. The feelings never came back. I felt displeased with myself for letting her think I loved her but really, I've never known love, true love at least. So maybe five days afterwards, I broke up with her and felt like crap. I'd always sworn to myself never to break a girl's heart and to always let them break up with me, but I didn't realize that sometimes breaking up is better than making her think you still like her. After that, I haven't had a girlfriend.

Last year in ninth grade I met the most beautiful girl I've ever seen. She had dark brown, flowing hair that sparkled in the sunlight and a face that can only be described as pure, but she also had the sweetest, softest voice and an adorable laugh. All throughout the year we would talk and talk and talk about little, pointless things, but it would feel so important because she would always say, "I love you" and it'd make me feel so special and so smart. I've always had problems convincing myself I was smart because I think a lot differently than other people, and she somehow convinced me that I am smart, and I believed it.

I thought I had everything at that point. She wanted to be a lawyer, and she'd talk to me about struggles she would have while in court and I'd just enjoy being the one she vented to. She was smart and confident and spoke her mind. We would call each other at night and bring each other food, and I thought I'd found the girl I wanted to be with forever. But one day it all washed away. I was very depressed, and she kept getting sidetracked when I was trying to open up to her, and I didn't feel like she was very interested in what I had to say. When I regained her attention, she told me, "Sometimes, people don't care."

That is not what you want to hear when you're really depressed. Of course nobody cares. I already felt that way and she had to validate it for me. So I got my backpack and just walked away, and guess what? She was mad at ME. The next day I could hear her breathing at an angry and annoyed pace. I asked her, "What's wrong? Are you ok?" and she said "No," and you want to know why? Because I'd walked away. To be honest, I was fed up at that point, but I held back because I cared about her and wanted to still be friends. But when I was apologizing to her, I realized she wasn't even worth it. She told me exactly this: "You disrespected me. No one disrespects me." Who did she think she was, the president?

At that point I realized that I had wasted my freshman year. I could have crushed on someone worth it. I thought we were super close. I waited for her after school every day to talk to her, and I would write her daily letters telling her how she made me happy or how my day went, and she wasn't even worth it. As Linkin Park put it, "I tried so hard, and got so far, but in the end, it doesn't even matter." At that moment I ripped up her daily letter and walked home. It was finally over. I didn't have to waste my time with her anymore. I actually jumped in the air and clacked my shoes together while on my way home. I was done with her. I'd moved on.

Nowadays I just sit at my lunch table with my good friend. We have a very interesting relationship that made us very close very fast, but I'm only 16, so what do I know? We met when my friend and I walked over to her, and the first thing that came out of my mouth was, "You look like you could use a friend or two," and she immediately smiled a great smile. I asked her why she was all alone, and it turned out that was her first year ever at a school. She had been home-schooled her whole life and didn't know how to make friends.

I used to think life sucks, but I know now that it's all good as long as you keep moving forward. People aren't always going to like you, and that's okay, as long as you still have friends.

A CROWN OF GEMS AND GOLD

Brandon Harris

ATTRACTION: I met this boy in the beginning of freshman year. I didn't think much of him at first, but as time passed, my interest in him grew. His body put me in a trance. Most people are ashamed to admit that looks matter, but I would've felt lucky to have such a cute boyfriend. Still, I looked deeper for other qualities within him. Unfortunately, he did drugs, did bad in school, and had an ugly personality.

VALIANCE: It was the midst of my freshman year and I noticed this boy because of how sure he was of himself and how he made me feel confident in myself. He walked with a solid step and had a calm, welcoming look on his face. I interacted with him from time to time and we got along, yet his homophobic views and jokes made me distance myself.

CHARM: At the end of freshman year, I noticed a particular boy that was … just different. His masculinity was so unique compared to other boys. Other boys are so aggressive when using homophobic terms, or just in general, but he was sweet when I talked to him. His presence had a vibe that made me want to be around him. Humility at his best.

AFFECTION: Sophomore year came along and it's a year I will never forget. This boy caught my eye at first sight. It felt like a romantic movie: two people, one place, same time. I felt so passionate about him. He's the only boy that made me feel this kind of love. When I thought about him I never thought about his body. I only thought about how I wanted his intimacy so badly. So I got to know him and eventually I asked him out. He replied, "I'm straight." That was that. I made sure there were no hard feelings or discomfort in our friendship. Eventually he moved to Mexico, then came back and went to another school. I lost contact with him after a while, but because of him I know how a true relationship is supposed to make you feel.

WONDER: The end of my sophomore year was like gazing upon my reflection in the calm of once-stirred water. This boy caught my heart because he reminded me of me. He wore a cute beanie in school and dressed like a player outside of school. He was very reserved in an innocent, self-assured way. He always had me wondering: Who is he? What is he like? It was at a school dance where I got to know a bit more about him. He was discussing how he and his girlfriend came to be. There it was: that attraction had to fly right out the window. It was just so shocking I didn't expect it. He had been so reserved that I thought he had a lot of secrets waiting for someone to crack.

COMMITMENT: It was the middle of junior year when I met the man of steel. Over the course of my attractions, I never thought about how true an individual would be to me, and I know commitment is something lots of relationships lack. We were on a field trip, and we went to a restaurant. I overheard him conversing about why he wasn't eating anything. He's Turkish, and part of his tradition is Ramadan: no eating or drinking during the hours of daylight for a month. He couldn't do anything but watch us eat our meals, but he did it with such resilience and passion that if you looked at him you would believe he was perfectly fine. It made me wonder what could he offer in a relationship. Could he be just as dedicated with a lover as he is with his tradition? I was attracted to him and tried getting to know him. I asked if he was gay, and he replied no and asked why. I told him that I wanted to have a gay friend to talk to. He replied with no offense taken, with a smile on his face. I got his Snapchat a while later but our friendship just faded. Although I didn't truly get the answer, I felt it in my heart: Yes he could have.

COMFORT: This attraction was sudden and unexpected. On the way back from another field trip at the end of junior year, I was sitting next to this boy I barely knew. While he was falling asleep he noticed me also trying to go to sleep and asked me if I wanted to lay my head on his shoulder. I didn't know how to respond, but I said yes because I needed time to process what happened. He was straight and had a girlfriend. An act of kindness is what it was. I'm so used to witnessing homophobia that it's the little things that count. While resting on his shoulder, I was still in shock that this was happening. After the ride I reflected on what I was feeling and realized that I want to belong in a place of ease, a place where I have no worries, a place of comfort.

All these attractions drove me crazy, and I wondered why. I wanted to forget about them all. I told myself, "Too many bad things happen in relationships," and "I don't need anyone to be happy." I asked myself, "What will a relationship change in my life?" I also wondered what's it like to tell someone you love them, what it's like when someone tells you, "I love you" with an honest heart. What's it like to get into an argument but enjoy the passion within it? These thoughts still linger, and my heart longs to sing the answers.

The boy that has all of these qualities will be perfect for me, worth the young love arguments, the distance away from each other, the mischievous behavior. Having someone like this will make me feel like royalty, like wearing a crown of gems and gold.

FORGETTABLE
Georgia Cienkus

THE CRISP, DUSKY AIR bit the tip of my nose as I climbed out of the smoke-infused cab. My ears suddenly felt the pulse of music from the red brick house in front of me. At the top of the front steps, the black door opened swiftly, nearly sending me backwards. "Hey. Everyone's in the basement," huffed the blonde who had almost knocked me over. Tossing her hair back, she led me downstairs, where cups and people packed the floor. I made my way toward my friends but paused when I met familiar eyes.

Suddenly I was 6 years old again.

I was opening a massive crimson door and hugging my sides, pulling my Hello Kitty jacket closer around my frame. I squinted at the sun peeking from behind the clouds, hoping it would come out and play. My daydream was suddenly interrupted by the crunching of leaves and my brand new hat being ripped from my head. A trail of laughter sprinted away from my furrowed brows and disheveled pigtails. Hands flailing in the air I scanned the horizon for the culprit. A pile of curly brown hair was crouched under the play set. Fists clenched, I stomped over to the little fiend.

"Caught ya!" I cried, jumping out from behind him. My freakish smile melted away when I was met with a widened set of dirty brown eyes. They darted every which direction looking for an escape, then locked in on the wooden castle. His nose scrunched the freckles on his face as he began to grin. He gave me a sharp wink, pushed me aside, and dashed off to his next hideout.

Swatting at my jeans, I scoffed at the nerve of this horrible fool! My jaw dropped when I saw my poor little hat waving off the top of the tower. "You can't catch me," he taunted, bursting into a fit of giggles.

Hands pushed my sleeves above each elbow. Who did this boy think he was? With all my strength I screamed my battle cry, sprinted towards the castle, and busted through the door. His playful giggling became a screech. My face burned with anger and animosity. Ripping my hat out of his grubby little fingers, I tackled him to the ground, pulled at his stupid curls, and punched his little freckles. Suddenly twisting my arm back, he rolled on top and planted a kiss on my lips.

"GROSS!" I cried, pushing him back to the wood chips. My final blow landed on the part of him that made me feel funniest: his lips.

Satisfied with my revenge I jumped up and smashed my hat over my wood-chip-woven hair. "Told ya I could catch ya," I huffed, unrolling my sleeves. My eyes almost came out of my head when I saw him lying on the dried leaves smiling back up at me. Those dirty eyes somehow seemed glazed over, softer than before. He sighed lightly while crossing both hands behind his head. "I've never met a girl who could wrestle me to the ground. You're pretty strong," he finally said, gazing at me.

My cheeks reddened as I searched for my next move. "Well, you kiss like a princess," I retorted.

"Do not!" he screamed, leaping to his feet.

"Prove it!" I yelled, so close to him that I saw his curls fly backwards from my breath. "Fine!" he stammered, pulling both my cheeks into him.

I shook my head, realizing that those same deep brown eyes were now gazing down at me.

"Hey, what's up?" he said, wearing that same mischievous smile. Blood rushed to my cheeks as he grabbed my hand. I had married these eyes twelve years ago on that very playground. Obviously it was make believe and totally illegitimate, but I couldn't stop myself from wanting to relive that little fantasy one more time.

"Yeah, long time no see, hubby," I replied, immediately closing my eyes and exhaling. I felt like an idiot. What the hell was that weird attempt at being charming? He probably thought I was so strange. I opened my eyes after the count of three and was surprised that he was still standing there smiling.

"You okay there?" he asked, slightly raising his thick brows.

"Yeah! Too much to drink," I lied with a plastic smile.

"Don't worry about it. Hey, let's explore the house," he suggested, lightly guiding my waist towards the stairs.

"Oh yeah, sure!" I stammered nervously, glancing back up at my friends who were obnoxiously swooning and flashing kissy faces behind his back.

As we climbed to the second floor, the pumping of the speakers grew softer as my heart rate increased. He knocked on the second bedroom door and hearing no reply let its hinges faintly whine and then creep back to their place once we were inside. The sudden darkness of the room left me completely blinded. Finally my hands met the gentle edge of a bed. I felt the springs vibrate under me as he sat down. Hands wrapped around my waist and pulled me in for a kiss. It was just as I remembered. Innocent and warm. He held my face for a moment more and we continued, kissing deeper than ever before.

What seemed like seconds of sheer ecstasy and familiarity turned into clothes scattered across the floor and a ringing. Ringing? An alarm. The sharp beam of light erupting from his phone pierced our dilated pupils.

"We should probably get back," he said, squinting at the tiny screen and tossing my shirt into my face. I couldn't figure out why we stopped. Why we were getting dressed? He, the one who used to steal my clothes, now wanted nothing more than for me to put them back on? Wasn't he enjoying it? Us? I tugged my shirt over my mop of hair and lightly ran my fingers across my cracked lips. He grabbed the door and to my surprise planted another kiss right on my drooping lips. So unexpected yet so familiar; so similar to those childish encounters on the swing set. I couldn't stop the smile that pushed through my jagged skin as his eyes opened and met mine.

"I'm glad this happened," I beamed, reaching toward his hand.

"Me, too," he grinned, grasping my outstretched fingers like a gentleman. He pulled away from the handshake for moment and leaned against the doorframe.

"You know, I feel kind of stupid," he said, scratching the back of his head.

I giggled slightly. "And why is that?"

"I never even asked you what your name was! Hi, I'm Chris."

THE QUESTION

Erica Lovera

Chilling nights, where we met once again,
getting high and drunk every now and then.
The way our eyes met
made me feel something I couldn't describe.

One thing led to another and I confessed all my wrongs,
and still you were there after so long.
We started talking again like nothing ever happened,
and I felt like my life was starting to get better.
We walked late at night
and held hands under the moonlight.
We told our stories and laughed, and I thought
it was impossible to fall in love with the same person from my past.
All those nights, whether we just chilled, walked, or ate
felt like I had the entire world right by my side.

The way you kiss me, hug me, touch me
makes me convinced that somehow you feel the same
and this time it isn't a game.
You are the only one who knows me well.
You are the only one I can be comfortable around
and count on when I'm breaking down.
It was hard for me to express my feelings because
I wasn't sure of the idea of us,
and it will be hard for me to earn your trust,
but the more and more I see you,
the more and more I want you
and the more and more I crave you

just for myself.
Call me crazy, jealous or a psychopath,
all I know is that my feelings grew stronger and even though
I cared what others used to think or say
I couldn't stand not hugging or kissing you throughout the day.

I thought bringing you into my house would be weird,
but everything was normal. I had nothing to fear.
You are so cute even though you disagree,
and I believe you are the most charming, daring, exciting, confident,
extravagant person one could ever be.
I know what love is because of you
I know what a friend is because of you
I know what it's like to care, listen and support because of you.
There's no meaning to my life if I don't have you by my side,
and I have no problem living life with just us two.
This is what I call true love
this is what I call a relationship.
I know what I want now
but am too scared to ask you upfront,
so let me ask you here in this poem
and please don't leave my heart broken:
Would you like to be my boyfriend?

JUST FRIENDS
Payton Gallery

When your friend asked you
Fuck, Marry, Kill at lunch
you chose to fuck me
and maybe that's because no one
ever marries just the body

I am the smooth indent
between hips and ribs
grand expanses of
exposed skin
bikini ties like present ribbon

You insist you saw my eyes
first, not my waist but
you are more familiar
with the taste of my tongue
than the sound of my voice

You seem to like it that way
fair—
My stories wander aimless
but your kisses do not
Both hands in back pockets
and skimming hair knots
skiing side slopes slow

I knew deep down
below the giggles
every time you pushed me
into the sparkling pool
how I caught you
the way I always do

Body bait is most effective
in the early afternoon
at temperatures above 70 degrees
A push-up suit is recommended
but not required; triangles
and string do just as well

I didn't mind then
being a body alone
I kissed you back
thought I'd never
see you again
so why not?

I wasn't mad that you would
fuck me and marry her
that day at lunch
It actually made sense
She was your friend
I was eye candy, lip candy
but we'd never be friends

LOOKING BACK ON LOVE
Michael Gonzalez

I HAVE NEVER BEEN in a relationship in my life, but I still like to imagine what it's like. I dream of someone who is not indulged by her vanity. Intelligence is also a must. I would look forward to having in-depth conversations with her. We would have similar interests and nerd out! She would be my friend. I would cherish her deeply.

During my freshman year in high school, this nearly became a reality. At the time I was addicted to anime, and I wrote some lyrics in Japanese on the back of my notebook. Eventually, the writing started to fade, so I decided to retrace the words in ink. While I was doing this, a girl noticed and told me that she knew how to do the symbols. Of course my ninth-grade self got excited, but I shrugged it off because I didn't know her that well.

Some time later, fifth period math class got new assigned seats with me and her sitting at the same table. We started class like any other day until I noticed her binder. It was a well-done drawing of the current anime I was watching. This time we had a chance to talk, and she turned out to be cool. She was really smart and good at drawing. When winter break started, we messaged each other frequently to talk about a show, ask homework questions, or make jokes together.

Luckily for me, eighth-period biology class began the new year with new seats, and I got to sit with her in this class as well. We started working more on projects. I finally realized that she made me happy, but I didn't know if she felt the same way.

It was very stressful for me. We would still text, but if I didn't reply, she would get really upset. I understand what if feels like for someone not to reply, but she was *really* upset whenever it happened. We would scold each other if one of us missed a day of school. I was still uncertain of her feelings for me, and I got sad when she talked to other guys. I envied their confidence. Even now I think: how can you be disrespectful and think that's charming? Or how can you only like someone based on looks?

At some point I told her how I felt about her, but she didn't feel the same way. My whole world crashed and burned. She told me specifically that I was only a friend to her. I was so confused by that sentence. Does that mean a boyfriend shouldn't be a silly, helpful friend? I guess she didn't want a "goofy relationship," which is what she called it.

But I guess that's what I want in a relationship. The kind where we can make each other laugh and be there for each another. Still, it was extremely uncomfortable to be in class with her after that, and I had so many classes with her. I didn't know what to say when we would walk the same way. She finally told me that I was ignoring her. I didn't ignore her on purpose, but I had accepted her decision and was looking to get over it and move on.

Around May, she texted me that she did like me back in January, but I never picked up her "signal." So of course my ninth-grade self got excited and stopped avoiding her. We chatted and laughed again, but I didn't know if we were something. I would ask if we were together but she didn't know either. Eventually I felt strung around by words.

A year later she decided to message me again asking if I still hated her. The answer was, "I never did," because that was true. I couldn't be angry with someone not liking me. Love shouldn't be forced on someone, and I accepted this. I still believe this idea And I still believe I'll find someone else to love the way I loved her.

"I couldn't be angry with someone not liking me. Love shouldn't be forced on someone..."

Michael Gonzalez, *"Looking Back on Love"*

THINK ON PAPER *about this quotation. What thoughts, memories, interactions does it bring to mind? What connections have you seen or experienced between anger and love?*

JUST WHO I AM
Calli Bilger

I HATE name tags. They're sticky, pull your clothes apart, and fall off at the moments you need them. Labels are like name tags, making you uncomfortable until you need them most, and then they're just gone. Looking back, I guess I was one of those kids who ignored labels and grew up not ever placing one on myself.

Middle school is where sexuality really shines through, where we start crushes of a serious nature, and where maybe a first boyfriend or girlfriend happens. I was confused in seventh grade because everyone was so concerned about having their first significant other and there I was just waiting to go home to food and my cats. I didn't understand why everyone so desperately felt the need to be with someone else.

In my first year of middle school, I did have a crush on a boy, Riley, but honestly never saw the need to date him. Maybe I just liked the idea of a guy that I could always lean on without having to worry about all the dating mayhem, although if he had asked me out I probably wouldn't have objected. There was also Elias. Everyone thought he was so edgy, and almost every girl wanted to date him but he was already taken by Cassie. Every morning before we were released to the middle school version of study hall, Cassie and Elias would sit together in the commons and look all cute and make everyone else jealous of their relationship.

I sat with a large group of friends a few tables away, still gross and sweaty from volleyball practice that morning, and listened to all the girls around me complain about how she didn't deserve him and how it should be them and, by far the worst, what they would let him do to them. But as the girls around me admired his curly skater hair and lean figure with the "prettiest eyes ever," I looked next to him. I looked at the girl with the fresh bleached hair and the confident smile etched on her face. I looked at the girl while they looked at the boy, and I found myself right then and there deciding to hide a secret not only from those I trust most but also from myself.

Freshman year of high school was hard. It was a big school with big people, and I was a small and shy freshman who didn't know how to make friends. Classes without anyone I knew from middle school made up a lot of my schedule, and those I did have with friends were so spaced out that I wanted to beg my parents to homeschool me.

I came home every day, had a snack, and talked to my parents about my day. At one point halfway through the school year, my mom asked me if I had any crushes and, well, not any that I told her. I had a crush on this one senior but I'm a realist and knew it just was not going to happen.

Sophomore year was a blur of getting into the swing of high school and making a few new friends, one of which was my best friend Emily. Emily brought back up the feelings from middle school where I felt something for someone that I thought maybe I shouldn't have. Emily and I became so close, holding hands and always walking each other to class, that it became an unspoken thing through the school that we were dating. We never asked each other out or anything and just ignored labels. People would ask us if we were dating and we would shrug. We made each other happy and in turn made ourselves happy, so we really didn't care what we were or what was going on.

I had math with her and one of our other friends, Sammy. When we were talking in class one day, Sam said he was bisexual. I had always thought he was gay since he only ever talked about guys and literally had said girls are gross to date, and I started to think maybe that was me, too. I started to label myself as bisexual about halfway through sophomore year and stuck with it and with Emily until junior year.

My junior year was the best so far. I made a few new friends, started hanging out with some old friends again, and felt like I had found my place. I was still super shy and awkward, but once I got to know people, I became my normal obnoxious self. I had lunch with Nicole, the friend who introduced Emily and me, and we started to rekindle a friendship from sophomore year. At the head of the table sat a bunch of girls in the grade below us. They would always talk about their sexuality as if it was nothing, and I longed for that confidence, for how carefree they were when they would talk about how their parents never put them down for who they were. Every time I heard them talk about their parents, I cringed. My mother's side would disown me if they knew and my dad's side, well, they might just accept me, but my dad doesn't believe in bisexuality. He said you always end up with one or the other and that's who you are, even if you are confused your whole life. He has nothing against any sexuality, he just doesn't believe in being in the middle.

I really have to give credit to Nicole for who I am now. She helped me through all of junior year in finding who I was. Since it was just the two of us who sat together during lunch, we were always each other's main focus. She explained to me the different types of sexuality she thought I might be. As weird as it sounds, I found it so interesting, not because it was about me but because I had honestly never given a second guess to what I was or am. Or how many different sexualities there are: demisexual, pansexual, androgynous, asexual, and so many more. It just amazed me that people had created labels to fit themselves.

Junior year, through all Nicole's explaining and all of my thoughts of uncertainty, she helped me figure out I'm pansexual. I love regardless of gender or sexuality. I love who I love and no one can take that away from me.

Well, I mean, Nicole is kind of trying to, saying I'm the most asexual nonasexual there is, but it's more of a joke. Now in my senior year of high school, I've reverted back to who I was as a child, to before the frenzies of middle and high school. To those who just don't understand, I tell them I'm pansexual, but to those who do understand, like Nicole, I am who I am. I do not put a label on who I love, and I am happy. This year I have taken my sticky and crinkled name tag back off and stuck it in my pocket to show only those who need it, because I no longer do.

DON'T
Izzy Dimiceli

DON'T FALL for someone you can't have.

Don't fall for the younger guy in your acting class who only cares about football.

And don't get too sappy and serious about it, like I am, because it'll make you feel like shit.

When he makes you laugh, don't take it to heart. When he does it a second time, hold your breath.

Keep your eyes busy. Don't let your mind wander, wondering how many ID's he's chewed through this past week or if he'd ever let you wear his jersey. The more your mind wanders, the more you obsess. Don't obsess over his full attention on the giggling girl who forgot her lines on stage. How he messed with her every second. Stare at them as she steals his stuff and he chases her around the room. Sure, she has a boyfriend, *maybe*. But it takes forever for him to answer your messages and he never looks at you that way. Everyone in class jokes about them dating. For the next couple days, be pissed off, full of irrational hate and crushing feelings you didn't mean to develop in the first place. Don't give him the time of day.

If he calls you pretty, don't call him cute. Make a comment about how everyone in your class likes this one exchange student, and squint as he says, "Not me." Don't assume he's dropping hints and that he likes you instead of her. Part of you will say he does, part of you will say he doesn't. Don't get your hopes up.

Glare at the girl he walks with in the hallway. Start a fight with your cousin's girlfriend, who you know has been flirting with him. Act like you didn't expect it when he tells you it's true.

When he messages you asking what you're doing, you'll think for a minute (again) that he likes you. Soon the messages start falling off, he takes a whole 24 hours to answer you, and underneath his name it says "Active 1 hour ago," but he hasn't opened the message you sent before then. You wonder, even though you told yourself not to wonder anymore, if he's ignoring you.

Take his script in class one day and read through it while he performs. You're surprised to see he knows his lines, and you stare, enthralled, as the stage lights bounce off his braces when he grins wide. He walks back to his seat and looks down at you, noticing the papers in your hand. He bursts out laughing.

"You actually knew some of your lines," you say, pushing the papers his way.

"I did, but he kept messing up." He nods in his partner's direction.

Laugh a little more. Let that moment consume your mind for a while. Let it poke and prod at your brain until it annoys you so much you don't want to see him anymore.

Don't forget to say hi when you see him at the football games. He'll do this odd thing where he stares when he sees you, and it'll leave you wondering if he really likes you that much or if he's just having a moment. Say hi. Wave. Smile. Giving him attention when you're around other people might be the only option left to get him to fall for you.

He isn't taking acting next semester, and you aren't sure if you'll see him in lunch anymore. Soon you're sitting in a ditch full of things you like about him, with so much dirt flying into your face it makes your eyes water.

Remember this isn't something to get upset about. You're older, so he should be the heartbroken one. Remember he's only a freshman. Remember you're going off to college next year, and attachment is dangerous. Remember how many other things there are to focus on.

Don't look him in the eye, or you'll trip right back into the ditch.

Don't fall for someone you can't have.

SIX LONG YEARS
Jazmin Carmona

⟶❤⟶

"I'LL TELL YOU everything, but don't laugh," I said.

We were huddled in a circle, knees touching. They looked up at me, their eyes attempting to read my story. My stomach dropped with a tingly sensation that ran up into my throat. "Ugh, I don't want to talk about it!" I'd been holding that secret for six years, and I wasn't planning on breaking the streak that night.

"Yes you do. We all talked about our crushes, so go," Mia said. Encouraged by our four friends, I clutched a pillow and started to tell them my embarrassing story.

"Okay, well, it all started in fourth grade."

"Woah, woah!" Valeria's hand dropped, spilling her juice on her lap. "You've had a crush on him since fourth grade? What's wrong with you?"

"See! I'm not going to tell you guys if you do that!" My finger pointed at Val, as I shook my head in annoyance.

Fay covered Valeria's mouth with her palm. "I'll slap her if she talks. Go!"

Cristina spoke up, not letting go of the Cheeto in her hand. "Guys, just shut up and let her talk!"

"Thank you," I said, taking in a deep breath. "Now where was I? Okay, so it was the second day of fourth grade…"

My palms are moist and my face holds droplets of that salty, nervous sweat. Staring down at my red-buttoned shirt I tap my foot, waiting for my mom to come back from the office. The smell of coffee creeps up my nose, as the long hand on the clock reflects against my tired eyes. Clenching my hands, I take in a breath, ignoring the quiet hums of the lady typing on her computer. I was supposed to start school yesterday, the official first day, but since something wasn't filled in correctly on a form, I'm starting today. At a new school. In a new state.

"No problem. We'll take her to class," says a woman with black hair and a welcoming accent that reminds me of my own and of my mom's. Black curls fall over her shoulders as she walks out, leading my mom.

"I'll see you at home." Mom gives me a kiss. I just want to cry right here, right now. After my mom leaves, I pick up my backpack and follow the lady up the stairs and down the hall. Her heels click against the shimmery marble floor, just building up my nerves. She seems to notice and slows down.

"You'll be fine. Ms. Alva is very nice. You'll like it here."

I just nod my head, not trusting her words. By the time she knocks on the wooden door, I feel like barfing, and once inside, having all those eyes on me makes me want my mom even more.

"Hey," Ms. Alva whispers, guiding me to the front of the class. I say a quiet hello before being put on the spot. "Class, we have a new student. Why don't you introduce yourself?" She walks away, leaving me exposed to all these kids.

Pushing myself, I say my name and that I moved here from Idaho. A few kids ask how it was over there and I tell them it's the same as here, only fewer buildings. They laugh. Once the little interview is over, Ms. Alva sits me with four girls named Marisela, Emilia, Cynthia, and Lucinda. During class one of them invites me to sit with them at lunch and play during recess. My nerves eventually ease, and by the time lunch comes I feel okay. My hands aren't shaking anymore.

Nevertheless, when I sit with the girls at lunch time they talk only to each other, completely ignoring my presence, and recess isn't any different. I just chase after them like a lost dog.

Val groaned. "Oh my god, I used to be friends with Lucy, but I stopped talking to her because Emelia, Cynthia, and Marisela hated me and they even told me so. Those bitches."

"See, that's why I hate them," I said, "because they were mean and ditched me. Even to this day I still hold that grudge."

"True, but Cynthia's makeup is so good." Mia showed us a photo of her from Instagram. Even looking at a picture of her boiled my blood.

"Anyways, so after they ditched me, I met him," I said, returning the chat to me.

He sits at a table behind me in class. He always comes to school very formal looking, with a vest and a tie or a white dress shirt. Since the moment I saw him and actually learned his name, I've thought he is the cutest boy. We both have the same chocolate-colored hair, only his is spiky like the top of a pineapple.

"Really, pineapple?" Fay leaned back against Mel's poster-covered wall.

"Because that's the first thing that I thought of, okay? Plus that was kind of what I called him a few times." I shrugged and shrank deeper into the mattress, happy in the memory. "Can I just tell you the cute things that happened?" I asked.

Mia nodded. "Yeah, sure."

We don't talk a whole lot, but the few conversations we have in between group work and me helping him are the happiest minutes of my life. He always radiates a fresh, minty smell, which is much better than the other boys. I sit three to four seats in front of him on the bus ride home, and when he's getting off I scoot away from the window and sit on the edge facing the small aisle. He always taps my shoulder or gives me a slight push as he walks past me. I make a face, mouthing to ask him why he touched me, and he just smiles before getting off the bus.

"You don't understand the amount of joy it brought me to see his face light up and to know that I was the reason behind that playful smile."

"Are you serious?" Melina covered her lips as she tried to conceal mocking laughter.

"Don't judge. Oh, and every time he walked by he left a trace of his smell."

"Aw, girl, that's cute," Mia said, shoving me. "Little creepy, but cute."

"I know!" I said. Reminiscing about all these things brought a sense of excitement, yet the gloominess wasn't too far behind.

"Girls, go to bed. It's late." The voice of Mel's mom broke my trance. She asked if we'd brushed our teeth, to which we all said yes.

"Hey, finish telling us tomorrow." Mia nudged my ribs, whispering goodnight to everyone. I whispered back an okay before drifting off to sleep listening to crickets, the only sound of the night.

By Monday morning all they did was bother me about who he was. They were their own little spies working on a case.

"Wait, he's in our gym class?" Fay said, looking up from her late English homework. It was fifteen minutes before 7:30 a.m., and we were sitting on the cool tiled floor in front of the library. No words were needed. My face told it all. "Who is it?'"

"The one with the Adidas and Nike shoes," I said, afraid for everyone else to find out my secret.

She thought for a moment then looked to her side, facing the lunchroom. "Wait, is it him?" She pointed at a tall guy with semi-pointy hair brushed slightly to the side, his neon sports jacket making his skin warm. He laughed with the rest of his soccer buddies, eyes squinting. Gosh, he was cute.

"Yeah. That's him," I said, making sure not to stare for long or else I'd start tilting my head and smiling like an idiot.

Mia's lips curled in disgust. "Him! Me and him hung out a lot before he became an asshole. Girl, why do you like him so much? He's horrible."

I shrugged. "Do you think I enjoy liking him?"

"Then why do you? I had gym with him last year and he's such a dick," Val said pointing her middle finger in the air in his direction. "He would never let the girls participate. Dude, I was open and he was right in front of me, and he still threw the ball to someone else."

"Yeah, I know he can be like that, but —"

Cristina groaned, pulling out her earbuds. "Didn't you tell us he called Fay a bitch last week for being on his side of the court? He's the bitch."

Fay agreed. I just stayed quiet. Everything they were saying was true. I knew he was a jerk and just mean in every way. But for me the boy from fourth grade, the one who played with me, was still there.

"Girl, look. If you like him, you like him," Mia said, putting away all her makeup in the small tinted bag.

The bell rang for gym, and the whole time I avoided Fay, who always brought him up. Even in the ugly gym shirt he managed to look like a Calvin Klein model, swaying his arms to the side before going to help set up the volleyball nets to start the period. His team against mine.

I swear I tried extra hard whenever I was going against him, but no matter what I did the ball went everywhere but over the net. Clearly his team was annoyed. They were mopping the floor with us, yet they gave us dead stares for not trying, which made me feel bad, and to make matters worse, he jumped over to my team to help us not suck as much. As he rushed for the ball he brushed past me, and my breath was cut short. I thought, *I don't need your help! Please leave! Leave forever!*

We lost and they moved on, but I didn't. My breathing was still giving me a hard time. *He touched me! He's still here!*

My vision started to blur as if a thin curtain covered my eyes. My hands started to shake as well as my voice. I started to sweat coldly and barely managed to stand on my own two feet. My stomach was attacked by a thousand needles. I remember my hands floating in front of me as I asked a teammate if I could sit out. My feet stumbled as I went to sit by the corner of the gym and hugged my knees, rocking my body back and forth.

Calm down. Relax. Breathe.

The more air I inhaled, the less I actually breathed. My hands were going numb and my heart was beating out of my chest. Before I knew it Fay was sitting next to me, telling me to control my breathing. Then the teacher and student leaders arrived.

I can't. Please leave. I want to be alone!

Their voices bounced off my head, and I started to cry.

"She's having a panic attack."

"We're all here for you."

"You need the nurse?"

God, just leave me alone, damn it!

My hands shielded my face from their eyes. The mascara I had applied just two hours before ran down my cheek as my throat felt clogged with nails. I felt someone wrap their arm around my waist and pull me up. Looking to my side I saw Fay's worried eyes. We started to walk. My breathing was still fighting with me. As we were about to exit the gym, we passed by him. He was looking at me, holding the ball in his hands. *Is he worried? Does he still care at least an ounce? Why does he have this effect on me? I hate this. I hate him!*

My eyes were still puffy and my nose red, but my friends didn't ask, they just changed the subject. I was quiet walking Fay to her class, and for the following two periods I did nothing but just pout like a pathetic puppy.

A loud honk and a red Toyota carried the senior homecoming court, waving their hands, followed by all the underclassmen. We got candy tossed at us and Val and I fought for it as Melina ended up getting more treats. I called my mom to come by the field and pick me up, and as I waited for the football team to drive by, my fingers zoomed into their faces, capturing a friend with the most constipated look.

Turning around, I stretched out my hand. "Mel look at—"

I saw him, but he wasn't alone. His arms were wrapped around her thin waist, pulling her closer. Wild curls bounced off her Nike jacket.

"You have to be fudging kidding me," I whispered, biting my lip. My arms dropped and so did my heart, as cliché as that sounds. The feeling I'd had a few days back with the panic attack was returning, the sensation of my heart pulsing deadly poison.

"What?" Val followed my eyes then cursed. I kept my eyes on him and his beautiful girlfriend. My lip started to tremble. He brushed her hair away from her golden skin. He smiled and looked up, and for a moment, I thought he was looking at me, at my glossy eyes burning with tears. Then he kissed her. Not a hard kiss, or a passionate kiss, either. Just a sweet, tender kiss, a kiss I'd always dreamed of. Even after all the things he'd done, I still wanted his lips on mine instead of hers.

"Hey, don't look." Mel tugged at my shoulders, but I couldn't stop staring. Once I saw he was gone along with the parade, I broke. I'd seen him with other girls in primary school and that ripping feeling only grew deeper with the years. I held it in, just as I'd been doing for six long years. After all that time his smile hadn't changed and neither had his competitiveness with sports. It's funny how I had his voice recorded in my heart, and just when I started to see his spiky pineapple hair, it all came back. The memory of us sneaking a chocolate in class or the day our knees touched on the bus. The image of his eyes looking back at me in my dreams.

A week passed and I still couldn't help but glance at him when he helped put up the nets, or when he jumped, fist in the air, when he won. Typing the alphabet on the laptop I listened to my writing teacher. "You can basically write about crushes you had, or anything with you in a relationship," he said, pressing to the next slide of the dull PowerPoint. I could literally feel my eyes shine when he said the word crush. They say that if you have a crush on a person for more than four months then it's not a crush, but you're in love. I doubt that I am, but there's something strange I feel towards him that no matter what he does, how rude he is, I still feel something. I can't explain it, really.

"You have until next Saturday to submit your piece. Start writing," the teacher said and clapped his hands. I've heard people talk about the six crushes they had, how they ended badly, and here I am with just one crush that's been shredding my heart slowly with every year that passes. Pulling the laptop closer to me I chose a font and began. "Okay I'll tell you everything, but don't laugh."

THE XY STORY

Cheya Washington

HIS NAME was X. He was full lips and green eyes, and I was curiosity and shy smiles. He was the kind of guy whose hugs made you crave him after the contact diminished. He would give you a gentle squeeze and a whisper that you almost mistook for him just breathing. X was simplicity and stupid jokes, and I was second guesses and insecurity.

I met X in the hallway of our school's music building on St. Patrick's Day. At the time, I was doing a show for my high school as part of the crew, one of the people behind the scenes, nobody important. X was sitting on the wooden bench outside the auditorium with a folder in his lap and his lips were moving, repeating the same couple of lines every five minutes. I was mesmerized, the sight of a cute boy making my cheeks warm. My heart was beating fast and I was a little too hyper at the time, the after-school buzz still fresh. I went up to him and tapped his shoulder and my heart slowed down and my brain went blank. When he looked up at me and smiled, lips stretched wide, my heart started thumping harder in my chest and I knew right then he was going to hurt me. He had long pale arms, with the legs to match, green eyes waiting to seize any opportunity, and plump, pouty lips.

I didn't know at that time that someone else was pining after him.

X had this way about him where everyone would flock to his open arms because they seemed inviting, safe. I found my own safety in them, but he was never really there to protect me. I was stuck in the spell he had over me. I hate to use the word "spell" like he possessed magic in his fingertips, when I was the one who held the magic and cast the spell upon myself. I was engrossed with the way my name sounded on his lips, or the way he would text me cute heart emojis. I'd never felt this way before, and I wanted our hearts to match the same rhythm.

Sometime in April I was exhausted from the long hours of theatre, and all I wanted to do was tell him about my day. It's nice to complain to someone every once in a while. But that night, my complaining turned into the words, "I like you." He sat there, shocked, big green eyes stunned with a hint of worry and mouth slightly agape. My heart was thumping against my rib cage and my legs were shaking because he was still quiet with his mouth open. When he finally spoke, he told me that he wasn't ready for a girlfriend, and I immediately told him that it was okay and that I could wait until he was ready.

That was the problem, though. I waited for him. I longed for him every day during the play's run. It got to the point where jealousy was clouding my mind, making me believe that everyone wanted to take him from me. Everyone wanted X, but X didn't want me. I invested so much of my time into him, from FaceTiming with him until the early hours of the morning, to obsessing over the way he would pretend I wasn't just a couple of feet away from him with my headset resting on my head. I wanted him to be there for me like I was there for him, but this required him to know me better and be a little more serious. For example, when I told him that there was a possibility that the man who I called my father all these years was actually not my father at all, he promptly replied with a joke, using a statistic about black children not knowing who their fathers were.

One day X and I were FaceTiming, each of us playing computer games, and I was talking about pasta and how if I ever had a boyfriend, I would want him to make me some. X never stopped playing the game and nonchalantly stated that he would be my boyfriend. I finally got what I wanted! But I didn't want my excitement to get the best of me. I still needed to make sure that this was the real deal. He said it was, and I fell right into the trap that I call our relationship.

It lasted all of 22 hours. Those were the hardest hours of my life. He walked me to class and left me with a chaste kiss to the corner of my lips, but the spark that I thought we had for each other was growing more and more dull to the point where I could see the wood from the match turning black. Then he told me, right by the stairs, that he wanted to just be friends and that he was sorry for everything he put me through.

I held my tears back and replaced them with pink cheeks and a tight smile. He told me that I was the best and that he was happy I could understand. I cried for so long that night, and he called me and I cried even harder when I answered. I could tell he hadn't thought it would affect me this much, that I actually cared more than he did. He told me he was sorry and I believed him, again. That night we tried sexual stuff, but only through FaceTime because the idea of our skin touching at the moment was too real and too much for us to handle. Nevertheless, I felt as though we bonded, but he said he never wanted to do it again. But don't worry, he reassured me that it wasn't my fault and that I was great. Why did I feel so sick to my stomach then? He broke my heart over and over, and I returned like a fool, thinking the next time would be different.

X was never good at keeping his attention on one person. Here I introduce you to the other person who was pining after him. His name was Y. Y told me that he wanted X, but I didn't want to fathom the thought that my X could like another boy. It didn't seem fair.

That summer, X and Y found comfort in one another, and X seemed happy. That's all I wanted for him, but I wanted it with me. I wanted him to hold me close and to be able to hold my hand in public, to call me his. But Y was home and his new security, and I was an empty shell and a shattered mind. This wasn't fair. I had done everything I was supposed to. I was his friend when he wanted me to be, patient and loyal.

The thing is, none of this matters anymore. X was confused about his sexuality and as much as I tried to understand, I couldn't. My shattered heart came first before the need to understand why he broke it. My emotions were like a carousel. They went round and round and round. I wanted consistency, but X couldn't give me that, and I don't blame him. But I needed my closure to finally let him go, and now I have it.

I KNOW
Maggie Palomo

SHE WAS WEARING pigtails. I don't know why this stood out to me the way it did but I always remember her pigtails. They were held up with those two plastic butterflies that had that awful smell. I don't think that repulsed me, though. When I first saw how she acted, I think that was when I started to dislike her. She wore a sundress. It came to her knees and was all white with tiny yellow flowers on it.

The first day of sixth grade was like every first day of grade school. What's your name? What's your favorite hobby? Favorite color? Rubbish, I thought. I was obsessed with learning. I know that sounds stupid and like a lie you would read in a college essay, but I really was addicted. The suddenness of knowledge, learning about the simple yet amazing world we live in, was my entire life. Learning was an art like dancing, and I was going to be the best. She was also obsessed with learning, but in a different way. My learning was about passion, but it was never that for her. Her learning was cold. She absorbed knowledge wherever she could, swallowing it. She let it settle in her mouth for safekeeping. Learning was a way for her to be ahead of everyone else. Her nose was buried in a book and mine was engaged in academic conversation. It was my flame and her ice. My passion and her analytics. My heart and her mind. I think that was when I started to really hate her.

How could this adorable, soft-spoken angel be so cold? The fact that she knew more than I did was infuriating. So much so that I made a vow to myself: I was going to be her friend even though I hated her. She made my blood boil and I made her face go cold. Even that very first day when we made eye contact, she looked at me with disgust and I looked at her with repulsion. We were not going to be friends, but I made a bet with myself and I would not lose to me. How do you even owe yourself a dollar? You can't.

I remember trying so hard to make her my friend. I think if she could have described me then she would have called me a barnacle. I asked if I could braid her laughable mess of curls. If she could help me learn more about the state capitals. Well into eighth grade I was convinced we would never be friends, and one day I asked her if we were friends. She didn't look up from her book when she said, "I sure hope so."

Thinking about it now I laugh, but things did change after I asked. I was invited to sleepovers, birthdays. I knew her family and even some cousins. I knew her better than damn near anyone who called herself her friend. When I fell for her, I fell hook, line, and sinker.

I drew her. I think that's exactly how it happened. I pulled out my wrinkled up sketchbook and drew her. The soft curves of her face. Her figure, or lack thereof. In my picture she was laughing, a rarity in the real world but in my head she would always smile at me. Her thin lips curled up and she looked like the sun. A tiny little bit of sunshine that I had held in my arms.

I could hear her laugh ringing in my head, laughing while saying my name because I made her happy. So yeah, I was freaking out because I was in love with one of my closest friends.

I didn't come out as bisexual until sophomore year, though. I wasn't necessarily ashamed, just sort of in denial. I remember coming out to everyone before her. My friends first, then my less than accepting parents, and then her.

I remember distinctly telling her, "I am bi." I played it off. I didn't want to make it seem like it was that big of a deal so I said it nonchalantly. I remember sitting there in silence while the movie played, waiting for her. I wanted her to react in some way. I wanted to see her feel. I could feel my courage grow dimmer as more time passed. We were just friends.

She said to me, "That's cool." That's cool? I knew it was cool, it was me; of course it was cool. But I wanted to know something else. Sitting next to her on that couch, hands almost touching, I wanted her to give me something back. Then she said to me, "I think girls are very pretty."

I didn't know what to say. I wanted to ask her why or say, "Really?" but a thick lump of self-doubt sat in the back of my throat. After what felt like ten minutes she kept her eyes glued to the TV when she said, "I think you're beautiful."

That was that. I was a goner.

She wasn't out, she didn't even have a sexuality. I knew that no matter what happened our love was going to conquer it all because no one had to know. In fact, when I would talk about her I would explicitly tell people, "I can't tell you who it is. She's not out yet." I carried our secret love like a trophy. No one had to know. Something I should mention is that we were not intimate. It wasn't that I didn't want to be, believe you me. She never wanted to be, always not ready or not feeling it, but that was fine. We never had to be intimate because I knew how much she loved me regardless.

It started off very slowly. I'm talking glacial. We held hands a lot, I put my hand on her shoulder, and she let me kiss her. Not very often, but I was allowed to kiss her. Every day she would tell me that I was beautiful. No one had ever told me that before. Being a big, butch, bisexual, I had never even considered someone finding beauty in me. Her words were like nicotine, and I was obsessed. One day, my hands had ventured under the back of her shirt, and my fingers were chasing up her spine. I kissed her very briefly, and I told her, "I love you." It didn't faze me when she faintly whispered to me, "I know." Maybe I tricked myself into thinking it was her deadpan humor.

A little bit after that, my friends helped me work up the nerve to ask her to be my girlfriend. I wanted to put a name to what we were. There was no way she could say no. So, in an act of unbelievable courage, I did ask her. And she smiled at me, and hugged me.

She looked at me with her big Bambi eyes and said, "Give me some time."

I was so sure that I had nailed it. I was so happy that I had worked up the nerve. Even if she said no, I had worked up the nerve. Go me. She smiled at me and hugged me.

She had me wait three months. It was agony. Happy and liberating, but painful. She wouldn't talk to me. She canceled movie nights. I tried texting her, and I told her before anything else I was going to be her friend. I suddenly realized that all that time, all that effort I put into fighting to be her friend might have been wasted. After the waiting period, she finally did contact me. In. A. Text. I wasn't hurt, though. She wasn't exactly the best with spoken words.

She texted me a quote. I don't remember what it was or who said it, but it wasn't her words, and I had more questions about her response than answers. The quote said something about a selfish heart and a person who wanted it all. I asked her what it meant. She said she was sorry. That from the moment things started between us she knew that she didn't want it to be anything. That she had been close to telling me before now. However, the feeling of someone adoring her like I did made her feel powerful. My feelings made her stronger.

I felt gross. It started in my stomach, and then I could taste it in the back of my mouth. She called it being selfish. Said she never wanted the commitment. She just wanted me to love her. God, did I. And after she told me this, she said, "If you can bear to see me right now, I would like to have movie night this week." The gross feeling moved to behind my eyes. It burned. Her frost and my fire had always been an alluring concept, but now her cold drained me. And worse, I wanted to give more.

After that happened, I remembered back to that first time, when we hugged and I told her I loved her, her face buried in my neck as she mumbled lazily, "I know."

HOW
Lillian Hua

WHO: an umber-eyed boy,
his tousled hair bleached amber,
a sap that fossilized my memories in gold.
him a half-revolution more than my twelve around a star
that still shines bright as the first time
I hummed Taylor Swift songs for a boy, pictured *Love Stories*
with him, the one who made me think I understood
why Juliet followed a stranger's very toxic trail
and that I could too. the one who blindly tolerated
my meek flirting and fervent denial,
cried from little things, kissed other girls, who
I let go, who didn't come back, the mockingbird I realized
had never been mine in the first place (and that his cage
of silver I'd been tending had been mine all along).

WHAT: his fingers on my sides like lightning,
zapping and gone, leaving me a burned, crumpled heap
of giggling and sooty winter jackets on the ground.
chasing and tickling until their teasing and winks started
and didn't stop, and was that why? we'd built ourselves on physicalities
—glances and grins, touches and timbres—so his brushing past
made a dark point I couldn't ink in,
our only colors being nonchromatic, electrostatic memories and
his touch left me weak-kneed.

WHEN: eighth grade, eighth period,
honors geometry, in a chipped old desk
beside a boy whose name I knew but never befriended.
between ironic springs and pointless graduations,

after the tired "erect a perpendicular" jokes,
during the quiet grins and crinkled eyes,
the circular weeks, the acute jabs,
the congruencies,
the nights searching across Cartesian planes
for answers but finding instead his name, and
before 2:32, learning that
three other girls filled his thoughts.

WHERE: room 207, the International Building,
in Hangzhou, Zhejiang, People's Republic of China,
30.252915, 120.075785, seven thousand miles near home,
stranded between warm rains and a pillow pet,
with friends and typhoon winds for company.
in gray hoodies and red flannels (did you forget? in China,
scarlet means luck, not passion), in the middle of our third week there,
caught in the start of summer and, of course, lost in summer love
stormy and transparent as the twisters outside.
on my bed cross-legged, with only histories and inches between us
even though we'd always be worlds away.

WHY: the conversations of everything essential (debt-to-GDP proportions)
while skirting everything important (him-to-me ratios),
the pun battles, the way I Met Your Mother, yellow umbrella in hand.
the athletes, the intellectuals, the futures
of this little world whose every broken state we can name,
the same periods ("race me!"), the same amplitudes (1.65m),
except our wavelengths never synced.
why I waited an hour that day, cold cheeks rusty as
the palpitating organ on my sleeve, gusts of thin wisps
like and unlike my breath curling before me, writhing slowly away
until it was lost amongst string lights and snowy street sludge
while I wondered about Christmas miracles,
wondered if wanting what I couldn't have was why I loved.

WRITERS THROUGHOUT *this anthology use structure in interesting ways. Lillian Hua uses the journalist's questions (who, what, when, where, why) to structure her poem "How." Brandon Harris uses a list of attributes in his essay "A Crown of Gems and Gold." Several other authors use juxtaposition, flashbacks, and short sections to create interesting tensions without their work. In the poem that follows, "Turning Green," Chelsea Ayorinde uses a pantoum, a highly structured form of four-line stanzas in which the second and fourth lines of each stanza are repeated as the first and third lines of the next. Notice how the pantoum's repetition creates a kind of incantation.*

Use an artificial structure to tell a story about a relationship, a love affair, a crush, or an interest. Don't be surprised if paying attention to structure paradoxically frees your imagination!

TURNING GREEN
Chelsea Ayorinde

Keith was carefree,
He always had new experiences to share
With bright eyes, he told me his crazy stories
I listened carefully, enjoying the lull and inflection of his soft voice

He always had new experiences to share,
His lips curled slightly to the left as he told another dumb story
I listened carefully, enjoying the lull and inflection of his soft voice
Deep brown eyes radiated with passion

His lips curled slightly to the left as he told another dumb story
About a girl he'd been talking to recently
Deep brown eyes radiated with passion
Slowly, I stopped listening to his stories

About a girl he'd been talking to recently
That's all our conversations ever consisted of
Slowly, I stopped listening to his stories
He hadn't noticed me

That's all our conversations ever consisted of
I became a victim of unrequited love
He hadn't noticed me
Keith was carefree.

SALEM
Bratt Chavez

IN THE SUMMER of 2010, I was walking with the homies in the streets of Albany Park, Chicago, on the way home from summer camp, when I saw a group of girls across the street.

As usual, my ignorant ass just thought, "Wow, look at those loud mouths." But I noticed one specific girl who was wearing a purple sweater and was quiet. I couldn't stop looking at her and trying to get a glimpse of her face. I thought I saw her face for a moment, but one of the homies called me and told me to catch up because I had slowed down and was bumping into people as I walked on the sidewalk.

I looked at my friend and told him to shut up before I turned my attention back towards the purple sweater. By that time the girl was far away and all I could see was her beautiful brown hair in the sunlight that came through the thick leaves and that purple sweater that was slowly turning into a smudge.

I stopped and stood there, looking.

I was in a big black hoodie, with the stupid hood on, sweating in the summer heat, but I just wanted to see that purple dot and enjoy its beauty as it disappeared into the heatwaves.

A couple years passed.

I got into another dumb school, in another dumb neighborhood, in another dumb advanced program, in the same angry city, and I was still the same dumb and angry brat. Just a bit older.

Freshman year I got suspended for making inappropriate jokes. I got my heart broken by a girl I thought I knew well, but it turns out she wasn't that great of a person. I was doing crazy things that were getting me into trouble and it was getting harder to talk my way out of them. Also, that bullshit called anxiety was turning into that other bullshit called depression. I was basically going downhill in life except my grades stayed on point.

One day in Spanish class, I was assigned to do a project with this really pretty girl. She wore pretty makeup (a bit too much in my opinion), red lips, dark eyeliner, and she had this birthmark that was really cute. I'd seen her before but my friends at the time were the kind of jerks that'd diss me if I even looked at a girl in a certain way so I was just always goofing, getting in trouble and just being mad disrespectful, especially to the ladies, and that's why I didn't even bother to talk to her during our project. I knew this girl was pretty and all, but I had to keep my grades up and just wanted to get the project done. Also, she seemed too pretty to be smart or nice or to even talk to a loser like me so I didn't really vibe with her while we were partners.

Sophomore year started and I was unhappy with my classes, my therapists, the stupid IB program, the weather, my so-called friends, and of course myself.

One day in the second week of school in Spanish class I was cracking jokes as usual, making the whole class laugh and the teacher mad. The teach told me to shut up or she would call security so I lowered my voice, but I stayed cracking jokes. It was quieter now because only the people sitting next to me could hear and laugh at my jokes, and there was this one laugh that caught my attention.

I turned around and it was the girl I'd done a project with in freshman year. Her sexy/beautiful laugh was the response to my vulgar jokes. I love to make people laugh because it makes them and me happy, but at that moment I didn't care if anybody else laughed besides her. Not to be perverted, but her laugh sounded like she was having an orgasm, but also it was innocent and warm.

I fell in love with that girl's laugh.

After that, you know how the story goes. We started talking more, we cracked each other up in class, we got into trouble together, we had fun. Basically, we became homies. This girl, she was so interesting and cool in my eyes that I just wanted to hang with her for the rest of my life.

Halloween 2014 was the first time me and her hung out, and it was dope. We clicked but I thought that a guy like me didn't deserve to be breathing the same air as this angel on earth, even if she thought I was cool.

One night we were messaging each other back and forth and I was pretending to be drunk while I was messaging her. She thought it was funny but she said she didn't drink that much.

I asked her if she smoked and she replied with a serious "No" because "It's bad for you." I decided to snap at her and tell her that she was wrong and that pot isn't bad for you. After a few messages I simmered down and she just said that either way she didn't smoke because she didn't like it. But then she said something that made my Grinch heart grow bigger than a healthy heart should be. She told me that she didn't like it when her friends were out smoking and drinking because it's not the smartest choice to make.

When she said "friends," I'm pretty sure my heart skipped a beat or two. Not only did she actually consider me a friend but she said she worried, and even though it was only in text I could tell she really meant it.

I was her friend.

I call this girl Salem.

About a week later I got some semi-great news from a classmate who randomly got on the bus with me one morning. This guy told me that he and some other people had hung out with Salem and they had a nice time. They talked and played games and my name came up in the conversation. They were playing fuck, marry, kill and it was Salem's turn and one of the names was my name.

What this guy told me next surprised me. Salem said she would've either fucked me or married me because she had a crush on me. This is the semi-good news because the key word here is "had," but all I heard at the time was that Salem could actually like a punk like me.

The next minute I did what Ted Mosby would do and began to plan how I was going to win over Salem's heart. At the very same moment I also did what Joel did in *Eternal Sunshine of the Spotless Mind*, which was to find out why she stopped liking me in a romantic way. The guy on the bus told me that it was because I acted like I didn't like her back and I seemed like a guy who would never date a girl like her. WRONG! I would marry this girl and spend the rest of my life making her laugh and be the happiest person in the world if I ever got the chance.

I also felt like a complete idiot for acting the way I did because I was the reason she stopped liking me.

For the next few weeks before winter break I acted like a better person, and I could see Salem liked that. My other homie, who we shall call Cheese, was great friends with me and Salem and she was kind enough to help me try and win over Salem's heart.

Cheese told me I was making good progress, but it wasn't enough to get Salem to like me back in a romantic way.

After winter break was over, I wasn't excited for school but I did want to see Salem's face again, and when I walked down the stairs to first period, there she was.

Her brown hair moved so beautifully as she spun around and saw me. She smiled her beautiful smile, with candy red lips, white teeth, perfect eyebrows, and there was a twinkle in her eye when she said my name and started running over to me.

I got off the steps and she hugged me.

I was the type of ass that didn't let anybody hug him because I wanted to give off the impression that I was a tough guy, but I just missed her so much and her hug was amazing. She jumped a bit because she's shorter than I am and I was holding her up.

After five seconds went by, I realized I wasn't hugging her back, so I quickly did. Ten more seconds went by and she was still hugging me. I was so happy, it felt like time had stopped. She smelled like summer flowers and felt warm.

When Valentine's Day came, I brought a chocolate bar for Salem, but I was too late. Another guy, who we shall call Tom Buchanan, had started talking to Salem, and that day he asked her out before first period. I saw it all, too. He pulled out a big white teddy bear with a red heart, some flowers, and a box of chocolates. I watched her eyes light up and the only other thing I felt besides my heart shatter into little tiny sad pieces was the chocolate bar melting inside of the wrapper as I held it in my sweaty palm.

A couple days passed and again I pulled a Mosby. I said to myself that she was happy and I should just pray and hope that she had a fun life with this guy.

This was her first boyfriend, and I watched her have her first kiss ever with this guy. Me, Cheese, and Salem were going to hang out and I could hear Tom telling Salem that he didn't want her to hang out with any guys, especially me. Salem said I was cool and there was no problem, and then she kissed him goodbye for twenty-five seconds. WHO kisses goodbye for twenty-five seconds? Me and Cheese watched from the stairs, and then Cheese turned around with watery eyes and said, "I'm sorry."

"Fuck that," is what I said, and then again that night after I said a little prayer to God before bed, I said "Fuck that. I want Salem to be happy but I will never be a quitter. I know this is the love I want. The love that makes me happy, the love that makes me want to be great in life. Somehow, some way I'm going to win over her heart."

A couple weeks later, Tom and Salem broke up.

After that, even though I was still trying to win her heart over I was just cooling because she was going through a breakup. But because of her I bought an electric guitar and I was going to learn her favorite song by the Beatles and play it for her.

When you break up and it leaves you sad, you don't want anybody hitting on you, and when Salem noticed that I liked her, things immediately became awkward. So I backed off. But eventually, I decided to confess my love to Salem.

It was at night, and I was wearing my lucky sweater, my lucky shirt, and I had my board on me. I frantically messaged Cheese because I was nervous and knew this wasn't the best idea, but I was getting tired and I had to tell Salem how I felt in person. I rode my board over to her house and hit a crack on the way there that threw me off, messed up my thumb, ripped my jeans, and tore a hole in my sweater. At first my superstitious side took this as a sign that I shouldn't be doing this. But then I said no, maybe this is the universe just telling me that you're going to get knocked down hard and it's up to you to decide if you keep going or not.

I picked myself up, dusted myself off, and gripped my bloodied thumb with a fist.

I rode over to her alley and messaged her. I used my thumb as an excuse and asked Salem if she could bring down a Band-Aid and some water. She said yes, and I sat on a rock that was near her house, right next to a parked car. I saw Salem come out of her house, and even without makeup and in pajamas she looked as beautiful as ever.

She smiled, said hi, handed me the napkin, and asked what I was doing here at night. I tried to make up an excuse but failed epically. So I told her how my thumb got messed up and why I was there. I don't remember what I said word for word, but I ended my confession with something like, "All I'm trying to say is that I came here to tell you that I truly believe I'm in love with you and I just can't keep that inside anymore because it really does hurt to be carrying around something like that 24/7." Then I laughed nervously.

She asked if I was asking her out, and I said that I didn't know and just wanted to tell her how I felt. She didn't know what to say and neither did I. She suggested that we change the subject for a bit and I said yes so the awkwardness could leave. We talked for an hour or so, and at one point her parents came from the store and saw us talking out in the dark. Even the dog came out to say, "What's going on here?" In the end her dad told her to come inside because it was getting late.

We said bye to each other and I said, "I really hope this doesn't make things awkward." She promised me it wouldn't, but the next day at school was harsh to deal with. She ignored me, and I just felt like a bigger idiot.

Months went by. I spent most of the summer in Mexico, and when I came back to the States I saw many messages on my phone and one of them was actually from Salem. She sent me a message saying that she missed me, and that really hurt to read.

I met up with Cheese when she found out I was back, and she told me a lot of things that hurt to hear. Salem was happy. She had dated this guy we'll call Malfoy, one of those wankers who knew my jokes were funny but didn't want to laugh because he thought he was better than me. This was Salem's first love, and they kissed a lot and dated for the first few weeks of summer. Cheese told me all of this and she also told me that even that pothead Malfoy said that Salem should probably be with me instead. Cheese agreed and then she also said I should move on from Salem, but she and I both knew that was impossible.

It was time to register for junior year and Cheese hit me up to go and register with her at school. When we both finished, Cheese got a call from Salem, who was also there. I saw her across the building's hallway and my heart dropped, goosebumps covered my arms and back, and I froze. I told Cheese I was going to go outside and she said OK. I walked straight down the hallway that Salem was in, and she was walking towards me. We both noticed each other from the corner of our eyes and yet we both kept walking. I hit open the door at the end of the hallway and sat on the ledge outside and pulled out my phone. Out of nowhere I felt these small warm hands around my face, covering my eyes, and knees touching my back, and I heard a beautiful laugh. Salem jumped down and said hi to me with a big welcoming smile on her face.

She looked beautiful like always but there was something different. Her brown hair was now a light brown with blonde tips. Trust me, she looked bomb, but she did look different.

She said, "What's wrong?"

I said, "Nothing."

"Well, why do you look angry?"

"I'm not."

Later in the day I hung out with my homie who was dating my other homie, Cheese, and he told me that Salem thought I hated her.

I said why would she think something like that? And he said that it was because of the way that I acted when I saw her for the first time after I'd practically disappeared for over a month.

I said I didn't hate her. I said that I would never hate her. He said "Cool. I'll tell her that."

But now that I think about it, maybe I did hate her.

The beginning of junior year was slow. I started talking to some new people, the classes were more boring with more work, and it took a while for me and Salem to start talking like best friends again. I didn't even get to take her to the Mexican ice cream shop, La Michoacana, that we both went to when we first hung out because she still felt a little awkward. But she did go to La Michoacana with this other guy we'll call Farquaad, and they had the audacity to walk right by my house on their way to the store and back. Farquaad was a major wannabee player who was always hitting on other girls, and he wasn't funny at all.

Farquaad was one of my many enemies for junior year because he would always try and flirt with Salem and also because I was trying to fix this one mess he left behind involving a girl whose heart he broke. This girl, let's call her H., was also dealing with depression, and since I had kind of learned how to deal with it, I decided to help her. We ended up becoming great friends and hung out a lot. She talked to me about things like depression and Farquaad, and sometimes I would talk about Salem. Cheese did not approve because Cheese is very stubborn and protective, plus she saw what I couldn't see at the time. H. needed a lot of attention, and she wasn't taking anybody's advice to get over Farquaad and focus on getting herself better. Eventually, I had to let that friendship go.

During that year I started talking a lot more with Salem, and when she went to Mexico the next summer, I gave her my old iPhone 4 that I listened to music on in Mexico. I made her cool playlists and wrote her a "come back safe" letter and asked her to bring me some pesos, and she did. She brought me back the pesos but not the iPhone 4.

Senior year was depressing because although Salem and I were talking like friends, I was kind of losing hope. By this point I was obviously just obsessing, but it's hard to not obsess over someone you love so much and who made you want to be a better you, spread love not hate, and who made you feel the happiest you've ever been. As creepy as that sounds.

I found out that Salem had a crush on this foreign student from Italy. How am I supposed compete against an Italian guy? I'm a fat, dark Mexican with so many issues. I look like George Lopez and this guy looked like a young Marlon Brando.

I was panicking because it was senior year and this was my last shot with Salem. I had to try and ask her out. All the people I got help from like Cheese, Doc, my art teacher, one of the school's security guards who knows his stuff, they were all telling me different things. But one thing that was the same was that if Salem said no and rejected me, then it was time for me to move on.

I asked Salem to hang out on a certain day, a windy day in the windy city. The sun was warm, and the sky was blue with a few clouds. We met at this bench circle at North Park University, where there's a flagpole and nice bushes and where I usually rode around late at night to clear my thoughts. I'd gotten her a bubble tea, and she said thanks, but she looked very confused at the whole situation and kind of angry, too.

I began to talk. I stuttered a bit at first but then the words just slowly came out my mouth. I told her this idea I had for a date where I would bring a portable projector, some folding chairs, a speaker, her favorite snacks, and we would watch a movie on top of a roof somewhere around our area. She said the idea was kind of corny, and I actually laughed and agreed with her.

But then I asked if she would let me take her out on any date, and just give me one chance to show her I could be a potential boyfriend. She wanted to change the subject just like last time, and even though I asked politely if she could just give me a yes or no answer, I let her change the subject. We talked about ourselves, and I had one of those moments where I realized she knew more about me than I knew about her. I realized that even if I did ever get the chance to be her boyfriend, I wouldn't really know what to do. But I knew that I would do my best to make her happy.

In the end I got friend-zoned.

She asked if I was mad, and I said no. I was actually not feeling any sort of way. It all felt like a mistake. I was numb again.

Looking back now, I've changed a lot. Trust me when I say that I'm not a punk kid anymore. I spend a lot of time thinking that I should've taken Salem to homecoming, I should've hugged her back all those times, I should've been more mature, I should've made her laugh but also shown her I could be serious. I should've run up to that girl in the purple sweater and said "Hey," I should've asked Salem out when I knew she liked me, I should've been a better me. At the same time, thanks to her, I am a better me.

I have big dreams, and I hope to change the world for the better someday. In the meantime, I'm in love with a girl I call Salem, and my story still hasn't ended.

YOUR EYES AND YOUR SMILE AND YOUR LIPS

Claudia Jiyun Zhu

I DIDN'T KNOW what I wanted when I stepped into our summer school classroom on the first day. My head was still asleep under the wet hair and way too trendy clothes. My mom had dropped me off and I'd waited until she left before I went inside. I was late, so I sat down and introduced myself in a voice that I didn't like with a name that never sounded quite right when I said it. I held my back straight and my head high, and I looked around. I hadn't seen you until then. Your eyes were down, but even so, I felt something.

Every time I have liked someone, it has been from first sight. I fell in love with the boy in the third grade with the strawberry blonde hair during recess, when he scraped his knee and I helped him put a Band-Aid on. Later I moved and fell in love with a tall, skinny, cross country runner when he broke the line of a race I helped run. But I guess that's not really love, is it? It's more like wanting, attraction. I asked you what love was one time, and you said that love is when you know you want to support that person forever.

I saw your eyes, your smile, and your lips, and I couldn't get them out of my head. I didn't pay attention in class. I just stared at you. You were from another school, a whole other league, a state of cooler people.

Somehow your number ended up on my phone, and I clicked send. Our conversations were interesting, and on the first night, you told me that I had actually made you smile. I blushed after that. I didn't know what to say.

Our texts grew both in length and frequency and washed away any remains of attraction I felt for anyone else. I told you about my life and you told me about yours. I knew that after summer school ended, I'd never see you again, so I hinted that I wanted to be yours and only yours. I told you this. We held hands, taking our friendship to relationship.

One night in the middle of all the sticky summer breezes and the thin sheets, I asked you what love is. And I told you I loved you. Not directly—in a very discreet, circumambulatory way. The next day, you caught my arm and pulled me in, and in that interstice between the wall and the doorjamb, you told me you loved me, too. We held hands and looked at each other, and that was enough. That was enough for me.

After we graduated, you had to go. You pulled me close in front of the open windows and told me you loved me and kissed me one last time. Your tears tasted like the rain, and my tears do now, too.

You messaged me one night and told me that your love for me was unique, that you would never love someone the way you loved me. Then why are you holding her the same way you held me? Why do you look into her eyes the same way you looked into mine? Why are you smiling at her like she's the most beautiful thing in the world and like you would do anything for her to be yours and like you would support her forever?

For the longest time, I wanted to scream in your face. I sent you so many flavored texts: sweet, to sour, to salty, to bitter, and each arrow of an attempt missed its mark. I looked at your pictures endlessly, over and over. I locked myself into the bathroom and cried, not from rage, or jealousy, or even pain, but just because I cared and you didn't care anymore.

Now I think of you late in the night when my phone and dreams keep me up. I think of you when looking at other guys and wishing they were you. I think of you when I go through our old messages and cry. I miss you, and I wish we could go back to the summer that was filled with your eyes and your smile and your lips.

LOVE IS EVERYTHING
Mike Arruela

———————— ❤ →

I got off the hospital bus and saw you:
My Chemical Romance shirt, Vans, blue eyes, orange hair.
My eyes lit up.
Seeing you made me feel like the pills were worth it.
Little did I know you would change my world.

What is love?
Love is ditching school and driving an hour outside the city just to see you.
Love is you coming to visit every weekend after school.
Love is talking on the phone for hours,
wearing matching band shirts, staring at each other,
seeing each other.

I used to write you letters and save my money to spoil you.
We'd go to McDonalds.
Once, your mocha spilled.
Once, you wanted to hold hands but you kept eating my fries.
Once, when you came to my house, you sat on my lap, and my mom
yelled at us.
I trusted you with my life.
You didn't care about how I looked.
You always made me feel safe, helped me have fun.

You came to see me when I was sick and we lay on the couch.
My mom yelled at us to get up.
We went to Dollar Tree and bought lighters,
threw them on the floor,
watched them explode.

We had a play fight and you said you would walk home
but you lived an hour away.

We planned our future together.
I wanted to spoil you but had no money.
I wrote you countless letters.
You gave me a bracelet with one word on it:
Hers
I wore it every day.
Sometimes, I still do.

You helped me get over my depression.
You slapped me when you saw my scars
then kissed my face.

Then you lost interest.
Our memories faded.
You treated me as if I was worthless,
stopped telling me you loved me.
But love is something permanent, even when the person is not.
Love is everything.

EXCHANGE
Jocylan McMillan

HIS NAME was Jay, and he was perfect. Those white teeth and dimples fit his face so well. His stature towering over mine was proportioned to a T. And his flaws were everything. Quirky laugh, lack of effort to spell. Even that outrageous temper.

I'm glad I never gave myself to him physically, but mentally he had all of me. He knew my past, he knew everything about me. From the little twitch in my nose when it's itchy, to the way I curl up in the right corner of my bed with my stitch stuffed animal, to just the way I think. He knew how my previous boyfriend broke my worth down. I was drained at only 13 and swore I was in love. I don't know if it was because I was bouncing from house to house or because school was a constant downfall or my family seemed to be against me. I felt neglected, honestly.

Jay promised me that everything would be okay. That he would never hurt me the way the one before him did. I believed him, and I poured my heart into him. One night after I left him, I lay there in his sweater thinking about the time we'd spent together. How attentive he was. His scent was still fresh, his voice still rang in my ears. I began to scroll on Instagram, and I had a notification from a new follower. It was his girlfriend. I saw the picture of him holding her just like he held me. His head in the crook of her neck.

It was crazy because he knew I was all his. I was crushed and lost who I was. Mentally I became unstable, couldn't think straight. How could someone promise me so many things and leave me with nothing? I was over "love." Physically I did everything so I wouldn't look like me. I went as far as cutting my hair, going on a diet, wearing makeup to cover up the natural scars and the beauty I wish he saw. I had been so wrapped up in what he fed my mind that I didn't look at the signs. Like how he never had time for me. Or how he lied and said he didn't really mess with social media. Or the time his Kik name changed to "I love Maya." I asked him about it and he said it was a bet. Just like the lies he told her about me.

I was so angry I hated him. I bleached and tore to pieces the sweater I had once cherished. The strong smell of bleach roamed through the entire house. I lit every emotion of anger, hurt, and pain on fire. I dropped the match onto his jacket, and the fire blazed and grew big. My perception of love was indeed changed, and my reaction to the men in my life became standoffish. I wasn't me for a while. I'm still not fully back to being me, but now I've identified my self-worth. I understand not everyone will love me the way I want them to. That people lie.

I've realized you can never change someone with what you tell them or how hard you express what you are feeling. People are aware of their actions, regardless of what they tell you. Just as the seasons pass, feelings change. But here I am a year later still dealing emotionally with the pain. I understand that I can't categorize everyone because of what HE did. Not every guy is him.

I found someone who I love, someone who also loves me back. It's an oddly functioning relationship. He's someone who tells me the truth and tells me when I'm wrong. Someone who listens and responds with the best intentions. A genuine person. I swapped out a liar for someone who enjoys seeing me smile. Someone who believes in me and isn't afraid to hand me his phone. Someone I wouldn't trade for the world.

IN-TRO-'SPEC-TION
Stephanie Galicia

ON THE FIRST DAY of school, freshman year, I felt naïve and tense among the strangers who were screaming and hugging. At lunch time, after grabbing my prepacked lunch from my locker, I was headed towards the lunchroom when a guy I'd never seen before came up to me with a huge smile on his face.

He quickly asked, "Are you a vocalist, or can you at least sing?"

I responded with a nod.

"Hi, I'm William, but I prefer you call me Will." I paid close attention to what he was wearing and the way he smelled. His white button-up peeked from the top and bottom of his crimson red sweater. I could smell the happiness of his smile, the outside sun shining on the trees. I was completely starstruck for a couple seconds and then finally, I responded back. "Hi, I'm Stephanie."

"Nice meeting you, Steph." Then he was gone.

As the days went on, I found him in the hallways again, and we started to talk. He gave me his phone number and we began texting. I started to learn more about his life, his music career, and his girlfriend. That last little bit of information made me squeeze on the inside and I decided to step back a little, repress my feelings. In the hallways I would find them arguing, his girlfriend crying, Will upset.

When I found out that they had broken up, I knew I had to step up my game by looking good, making an impression, trying to get his attention. I would come up to his locker every single day, and we also hung out a couple times. I found out more about him, and every single time I would notice his smile and that he was only smiling when I was around.

After a few weeks he stumbled upon the question of me being his "girl," and of course I said yes. It happened during the weekend, and I was super excited to tell my friends, the school, and the whole world that I was in a new relationship that would change my high school view. That week was probably the best. He wrote me a song and sang it in front of everybody. He even told everybody about our relationship, people that I didn't even know. People called us cute and he would walk me to class, ask me about my day. Whenever I was around him I just wanted to kiss him, hug him, and tell him how he made the world seem pink. I felt adored and just so content about everything. But at the end of the week, my happiness was cut short and I stopped smiling.

"He broke up with me so early," I remember telling myself. In the worst way, too. It started with him texting me during my class telling me that we "had to talk." At that very instant I knew that it wasn't good.

After school I didn't feel like talking to him face to face, so I went to his locker and said that we could talk later that night and went straight home. When he called, I got the whole explanation of why he didn't think our relationship would work and my heart just completely shattered. I think for just a small moment I went hysterical. First I started crying, then anger just started to rise inside my body. I was infuriated at the lies he had told, and at how broken-hearted I felt.

The next day I didn't want to go to school. Once there, I felt like just pushing mute and not hearing the sorrow and pity people had for me. My feelings were just rage and regret. I eventually had to be picked up from school because I could think of nothing but him. I went home and let all my feelings out. I screamed, I cried, and eventually took a really long nap so that thoughts wouldn't haunt my mind, but I couldn't stay like that forever. I had to see his earth-brown eyes and smell his deep scent of petrichor when I passed him in the hallways. I started to think to myself, was I in love with him? Or was it puppy love?

"It was only a week, how could I have possibly been in love?" I thought. And I didn't get past this question for a couple of weeks because it was still hard to talk to him without stuttering, still hard to think about him without smiling, still hard not to lock myself in the bathroom and cry at the thought of him. I mean, could I love him? I'd never felt this way about a certain person and the pressure of adults and of the media that "teens can't love" made it harder to know if I was in love. The thing was, I hadn't fallen in love within that one week we were dating. It was the whole experience of getting to that part that I fell in love with. But a few months later, I figured out that I was just in love with being "in love." The way I figured that out was pretty interesting, though, because it was two months after we dated.

He asked me to go to the theater as just friends. When I got there and saw him, I don't know what happened, but I instantly felt a deep remorse and realized that I no longer missed him, just the memories we shared. He smiled at me, but it didn't feel the way it used to. Instead of smiling back, I just looked away and I was like that throughout the whole date. He constantly tried holding my hand or putting his arm around me like in those cliché movies. He felt like a buzzing bug that I just wanted to swat. All I wanted to do was watch the movie. He would kiss my cheeks, try to make me cuddle against him. When I would look at him, I didn't feel anything, but then I would think about how it was when we first went to theaters and in a way I sort of smiled, but I only thought about the first experience of going to the theater with him. I couldn't stand him anymore. There was no more happiness with him. I excused myself and left him, mid-movie, alone. I was happy and felt accomplished in a way.

Right then, I knew that I hadn't been in love. Now I'm not so sure. Maybe I was in love and then moved on. Was it my first love? Possibly. I've even asked my parents about how they knew they were in love, and they said that they just knew. I'm not so sure. But one thing I do know is that it's possible to fall in love with the thought or the idea of love and there is nothing wrong with that.

WRITE ABOUT A TIME *when you were disappointed by love or found yourself "in love with the thought or the idea of love," as Stephanie Galicia writes in "In-tro-'spec-tion."*

Her essay ends with "and there's nothing wrong with that." Was that true for you, too?

PHOENIX

Juan Manuel Sandoval

I cry out your name
across the distant ocean of sheets
but all I hear are echoes and
laughter. Is this all a joke to you?

My only friends
are these four walls and the could've beens
my only company
the shadows of a man who used to be.

I try to break through to you,
hitting my love against your steel cage
but time runs off the clock.
I drag my feet across linoleum tiles,
my reflection in the magic sheen,
hues of black and blue. I'm the dust
left after the curtain closes
to our silent night.

I want to be a part of something bigger,
want us to smile and kiss like in all those pretty pictures
but as I'm holding on with white knuckles
epiphany rises from the waves
and a gentle voice whispers:

You're gonna be all right
You're gonna be all right
You're gonna be all right
Just gotta make it through another night.

My voice gets a little louder
as I stand my ground, but you storm
in like rolling thunder
all immensity and threats.

You crush my heart with your paws,
throw me into the corner, against the wall
insisting that no one else will take me.
If I fly away, who else will want me?

I believe you,
scurry away like a mouse.
I believe you,
cower in the sheets.

I could get up get up
but my bones feel like dust.
I cry, both mad and afraid
as the tears turn into particles of hate.

But I want to be a part of something bigger.
I turn the faucet on and wipe away the evidence of pain.
I can see the sun rising and hear that voice, louder this time:

You're gonna be all right
You're gonna be all right
You're gonna be all right

You're gonna be all right
You're gonna be all right
You're gonna be al lright

From the dust I shall rise
From the dust I shall rise
I'm gonna be all right.

SOULMATES
Rachel R.

MY LAST BOYFRIEND'S name was Matt. I thought I loved him, but you can't *really* love anybody you've only known for three months.

We met at a party at my friend's house. It was our usual get together: we play Cards Against Humanity, eat two pizzas, goof off, and *maybe* watch a movie. Since we call it movie night.

Matt was a stranger. He went to school with my friends, and he had grown on them enough to be invited. Prior to the party everyone had told me he was really sweet and was worth a try, and I was planning on being immediate friends with the guy. I'm not usually an outgoing person, but I can't control my excitement during parties like this.

I walked in the door and everybody greeted me with the usual aggressive hugs, and I got a wave from the new boy.

"Look who finally showed up," Omar sassed.

"Look who finally came out of the closet," I laughed, gesturing to his boyfriend sitting next to him on the couch.

"Shut up," he hissed through a smile.

I rolled my eyes, walking over to a friend who was playing the piano. We both said nothing, but I occasionally pressed a random key to get her attention. She grinned at me and swatted my hand away. Behind me there was suddenly a commotion.

Another one of my friends, Amy, was making jokes about Matt, who was now wearing a bright pink wig on the top of his head. It contrasted harshly with his jet-black hair and caramel skin tone.

"You look so hot," Amy joked, patting the wig down on his head. He looked absolutely ridiculous.

My jokester senses tingled, and I bounced over to this new kid. I looked him directly in the eye, with a completely straight face, and firmly set my hands on his shoulders.

"Oh my god. Fuck me," I said. I was joking, of course, because you don't just say something like that to someone you just met.

But his eyes widened and he turned bright red. I turned away from him, laughing. I had really gotten him. I was the funniest person in the room. I was a comedic genius.

He did not laugh; he walked away, and sat down, lips pursed and hands pressed together in front of his face.

That was it. That was the beginning of the end. I had started something with no intention of doing so. My comment had gotten to him, pulled at his heartstrings, and made his brain all fuzzy. The idea that I could make anyone feel that way made my heart stop.

The rest of the night was full of weird longing looks and awkward cuddling. My friend Omar had vowed that Matt and I would end up together if it was the last thing he did. I thought: what the hell? I'm not interested in anyone else right now. Why not?

Big mistake.

Our relationship started with a terribly inexperienced make-out session in a closet. It was like a movie scene. All our friends pushed us into the small room and wouldn't let us out for at least 5 minutes. We ended up playing patty cake and talking about our feelings since we were trapped. Then, after we slinked awkwardly back into the room full of friends and strangers, Matt nuzzled into my neck and asked, "Where have you been all my life?"

"Waiting for you," I replied in the sappiest voice I could muster.

By the time two months went by, I had convinced myself that I was actually falling for him. He was so nice to me and he seemed dedicated to the relationship. We talked every day over Facebook or Skype, sometimes just sending each other cute lovey-dovey stickers and emoticons. During the summer, we had dates at the local park, where we would hang out and flirt *incessantly*. Each time we would leave disheveled, emotionally and physically. My life revolved around him. During school I'd doodle thousands of pictures of us together, recreating our silly conversations and comments we had made. I didn't think he was perfect, but I really thought he could be the best thing in my life.

Just around the time I started thinking that, Matt messaged me on Facebook and told me we needed to talk. He had been in Florida visiting his mom all week, so we hadn't been able to have a conversation. I definitely agreed we needed to talk, but he meant it in the worst way possible.

He wanted to break up. He was losing the spark and claimed he didn't love me anymore. I found out later he was never even attracted to me. The suffocating realization of all the lust and puppy love made me feel sick. How could he say all those things to me and act like he really cared when he didn't? I should've realized it sooner, because he was always trying to fix me. It was like he had an obligation to make me into a better person. How can some dumb boy who's only known me for three months try to fix me when he doesn't even know me? I was furious, everything hitting me at once. But I didn't yell at him. I just let him go and never talked to him again.

That's why I hate having crushes. And I hate getting into relationships.

Everybody always acts like love is the greatest thing, like it's a weird trend that never goes away. People are constantly asking if you have a boyfriend or a girlfriend, asking if you like anybody, like it's the most important thing anyone can think of.

It's actually nice being in love, I'm not going to lie. I see what all the hype is about. But people forget to mention that it's only good when it's reciprocated, and someone loves you as much as you love them. That's what everybody is raving about. But I've never had that, not in a romantic way.

I love my friends. My best friends. My squad. They love and support me when no one else will. We're like a family. We even have little disagreements. We just never let them break us apart. Even the most intense arguments end in a comfortable resolution. When we disagree, we agree to do it.

During all the mess of dating Matt, they voiced their concerns about him. My one friend, Bri, hinted a lot at how uncomfortable he made her. They were friends at the time, but he had made negative remarks about her appearance more than once. Since she has a similar body type to mine, this concerned her. How could he be dating me if he thought she was ugly?

Amy stayed friends with him long after the break-up. I was convinced she might even end up dating him. But she, too, was hit by the bus of reality one day.

Now at movie night, instead of cuddling with a dumb boy, I cuddle with my best friends. They've always been there for me during the hardest times in my life, and I've been there for them as well. I've never experienced true romantic love, but the love I get from my friends is the strongest and most important love I've ever felt. And the love I feel for them is just as strong. If I could marry my friends, I would. They're the true missing puzzle pieces. My real soulmates.

People aren't joking when they say sisters before misters.

EVERY CRUSH IS THE ONE

Grace Yang

OF COURSE I had seen Noah before in the hallways or slamming balls into the goal on the soccer field. When he was not outside, he and his group tossed paper airplanes in the library, looking boyishly excited.

I was a senior in high school, a year away from eighteen and ready for my life after graduation. By now, I had gone through enough life-threatening assignments to be called a veteran by my underclassmen. I felt very competent and at ease with myself. My rhythm had yet to be broken until one day while I was scribbling down notes from the chalkboard, something light swatted against the back of my head.

I turned around to see Noah, his arm slightly arched and his expression cool. When I faced back toward the chalkboard, I felt another paper ball knock the back of my head and heard his suppressed laughter.

So yes, on first impression Noah was not enthralling. He had the look of a misfit with his teeth always flashing from a smug grin and his hair peeking out in dark tufts over his forehead. If he had played a character in a movie, he would have been the bully in the cafeteria, the one that ended up with a pie in his face.

I managed for the boys' soccer team on Mondays, which involved carrying water for the boys, taking statistics of their goals, and doing my homework on the bleachers. The guys weren't very interesting, even during the rare times when they played shirts versus skins. I had only really looked at them once during the season and that was while the boys were scrimmaging, one of the blurs racing after the ball skidded to the ground and a very human *oof* followed.

I saw Noah on the grass, our eyes meeting briefly as his mouth pulled into a half smile, half grimace. I was about to stand when Coach gestured at the two girls next to me. Noah slid his arms over both of their shoulders and they helped him walk back into the main building.

The next day I was alone in the library in full homework mode, my headphones plugged into both my ears to signal a warning: I'm busy! My high school was heavily academic, the kind of pre-college, prestigious boarding school that you had to apply to attend. In my first year, I had bugged all of my friends during their breaks, hoping for any airheaded tidbits of gossip. Now, after a hard knock lesson in failing two classes in the same semester, I only reached out when it was convenient and I always studied efficiently before tests.

Over my music, I heard a voice. "Hey, did you do the homework?"

I was surprised to see Noah scooting into the seat next to me.

"Well, he did say he would collect it today," I replied.

"Oh."

I might have been a tightwad about finishing my work on time, but I wasn't stiff about who was allowed to see it. I pulled out my binder and let Noah copy. Actually, it was the first time someone had come up to me for anything academic and I peeked at him while his face was turned down toward the table.

"Is your leg okay?" I asked.

"Sure, I'm going to practice today."

I tried to muster something from my brain besides small talk babbling. "Sorry I won't be able to see you score goals today. I've got a major paper due."

Noah stopped writing to look at me. His expression was sly. "So, how come it wasn't you that helped me back to the nurse?"

I shoved back the burst of embarrassment I felt meeting his gaze. "That was Coach's decision which girl to help you back, not mine."

"Hm." He stood up, sliding his bag over his shoulder. "Well, thanks for saving my life on this worksheet. I'll see you later."

After that, Noah went out of his way to invite me to his friends' study sessions. Every day before class began, he would tap the back of my head, asking me to dare him to ditch. The one time I actually did, he asked the teacher to go to the bathroom and came back in the last five minutes of the period.

Mr. Williams paused from writing on the chalkboard and shot him a look. "What took you so long?" he asked.

Noah shrugged, casting me a small grin as he spoke. "I got hungry on the way back and grabbed lunch."

The rest of the class gawked and I had to stifle my laughter into my palm. Seeing his mouth twitching like that, I knew that I was doomed.

Noah wasn't good looking in an ache-your-heart kind of way, and he definitely wasn't top of the chain in terms of popularity, but once I noticed him it was hard to stop. Beside the goof-offs he had with his friends, the little things became more apparent to me. Like the way his loud laughter would transform into something a little more embarrassed when he and his friends were chewed out by the teachers. A number of would-be dull classes were made fun when he injected a joke into them.

Noah wasn't my first crush, but he was as important as all the others had been. Like any girl, I went to my best friend and waited for the giggles and blushes that would usually come from mentioning a boy.

Miranda was one of shorter girls at school, but she was witty and extremely quick-tongued when she was angry. More importantly, she held residence as someone whose opinion mattered to me. What I did not expect was for her to roll her eyes and dismiss my confession with, "He's shameless."

"He's honest."

"He's always messing with the teachers."

"It's funny."

"He's a *dick*," she said, emphasizing the last word. "You're not seriously considering him are you?"

I opened my mouth once and then closed it, feeling my expression grow cold. I did not like it when other people, even girls from my pack of sisters, insulted boys I had branded as special.

All of the descriptions Miranda had used to describe Noah, minus the last, were characteristics I liked about him. He was refreshing, different from most of the boys there, who were so self-conscious that any joke you made at their expense seemed to come out as an insult on their end. In fact, what I hated most about an academic-based school was that everyone was so serious about their futures. The few times that you got to stop and take a breath, like a normal teenager, you felt guilty.

Noah had a lot of the adventure and energy that I had given up searching for in my high school career. I had gone from being the pride of my old school to being one of the worst students, on the verge of being kicked out for having lame grades. As long as I was at this school I could never forgive it or myself for putting me at an all-time low. When I was laughing at Noah's jokes, my stomach didn't hurt quite as much and my head didn't feel as heavy.

That was until the letters from Champaign came rolling around.

The University of Illinois Urbana-Champaign was the shoo-in school. The majority of the senior class applied every year to the point where it had become a reoccurring joke among my classmates. The Friday that their website updated our application status, my class spread an invitation for a gathering to share their acceptances with each other.

Right after my last class ended, I holed up in my room alone to check my status. When I opened the page, I retraced the small print over and over. A cold feeling washed over my gut each time. Deferred.

The next day in all my classes, I tried to make myself small and inconspicuous. The fact that I felt shaky about my chances of getting in was no secret and my classmates had enough tact not to touch the subject. The only thing I had to fear was the small landmines made by talking with an oblivious classmate.

"So, which school did you get into at Champaign?" Noah asked before I had even set my bag down.

"About that." I swallowed hard, feeling the uncomfortable whispers of not being up to par creep into my ears. "I actually got deferred."

There was a brief pause as he processed this. I had to give him some credit. For someone with his tendency to burst out the first thing he was feeling, Noah was doing well keeping his emotions contained.

Finally, he blew his bangs upwards out of his eyes and said, "Come on, that's not a rejection. It's an extended waiting period. By the time February rolls around, you'll be in."

"Right."

"Hey," he said, kicking my leg lightly under the table, "both of us should aim for getting C's in this class."

He was talking about nightmare scenarios now like they were rare candies. "Um."

"C for Champaign is lame," he said, smiling wide.

Even if I didn't totally get his logic, I did understand one thing. He was trying to cheer me up.

The second time I mentioned Noah to my friends, it was to another boy. Eric and I had been tight for three years. We knew each other's quirks and we had settled comfortably in a zone of no awkward feelings. His common greeting for me was *duuude* and sometimes this was nice, because it was a reminder that Eric and I practically lived on the same page. Other times it felt like a pinch to my girlhood.

"You like Noah?" Eric said. To my relief, he did not sound nearly as scandalized as Miranda had. All the boys at my school were wound together on a similar wavelength.

"Right," I affirmed.

"Why?"

"He can be sweet when he wants to and he's funny."

Eric's eyebrows rose incredulously so I added a line he would better understand. "And he's cute."

"I'll agree with that," he replied thoughtfully. "He definitely doesn't get his clothes from Walmart."

"You're pretty close with him," I ventured.

Eric rubbed the back of his neck. "Sure. He doesn't talk much about girls, though, and when he does, I don't think he actually knows what he's doing with them."

"Has he mentioned me?" I asked.

"No." At my downtrodden look, Eric quickly amended himself. "I mean, last time I talked to him was soccer season, so things might have changed."

I thought about my conversation with Eric for a while after. I had kept my ear open for gossip throughout my entire high school career, and beyond Noah playing a goof in class and around his friends, I had yet to hear the romantic side of his dirty laundry. That changed a couple days later.

Both of us had come to class early and were waiting outside the door. I checked the time on my phone: five minutes until the period started. I had loaned my laptop to one of my teachers to clean the files and I had the time now to pick it up.

"Where you going?" Noah asked.

"Math office," I told him. "Want to come with? It won't take too long."

"No," he said, but he was following me anyway.

I smiled a little. "So, Eric was complaining because his parents always keep us in the living room when I come over. Have you ever had a girl over at your house?"

He rolled his eyes a little. "I'm not that much of a loser. Allison's come over a few times."

I perked up a little. I knew Allison. She was top of the food chain in terms of popularity for the girls and completely gorgeous at that. It was not her status that had caught my ear, though. Noah had referred to Allison's name with the same awkward tone I used when I was embarrassed about mentioning an ex-flame.

"Did you like her?" I asked.

He made a face. "We don't need to talk about that."

I had known him long enough by this point to understand that anytime he shrugged off a topic, it was an embarrassing one for him. I didn't pry. At the very least, I knew he was capable of liking girls now.

My first try wooing him was with Matchomatics. You took an online quiz courtesy of our class club and paid two dollars to print out a list of the people you had matched with, fifteen girls and fifteen boys. No one took it seriously, but every year on Valentine's Day, there was a horde of people lined up by the table.

I had all but forgotten about Matchomatics a couple classes later, until Noah pulled his list out next to me. He was bored again.

I motioned for him to pass me his list and read through the names carefully. Lo and behold, there my name was, at the very bottom of the page, but still there. I took my pencil and circled it.

He took the page back and paused at my name. My heart was beating against my ribcage when he finally said, "Well that's interesting."

That was disappointing, and so were all the times I went out of my way for him after. For all the nice thoughts I had about a Prince Charming whisking me away, I wasn't a complete moron. Each time I had had a serious crush on a guy, I always made sure that I was prepared to be met with open arms or to be rejected. What I hadn't anticipated was for Noah to blink and laugh the way he did when I asked him to walk back to the dorms with me or to do a small favor.

As it turned out, I didn't need to go through all the trouble anyway. His answer came in the form of high school prom.

In terms of our school's culture, PROM (wow!) was a big-time bash. Most of the high schools that I knew rented a hotel for the night, but not mine. My senior class club had spent the past three years fundraising to build up for renting out a night in Chicago. The location was perfect. All I and the majority of my girlfriends needed was a date.

As Noah and I were walking back to the dorms, the topic came up.

"You have a girls' prom dress page?" Noah exclaimed.

"Sure," I said. "Otherwise a couple of us might end up getting the same one."

"Can you show it to me?"

"I'd rather not. I wouldn't want you to see your girl's dress early." I jabbed his side playfully, and he rolled his eyes.

"What, it's like a wedding now?"

"Sure." I hesitated. "Who do you want to go with, by the way?"

He shrugged. It was a question that he had encountered many times by that point. "One of my guys is hooking me up with someone."

Not me. For a second my heart stopped. I felt cold. "Oh?"

"Honestly, prom is such a pain. Who are your eyes on?"

I looked at him for a beat too long. "You don't already know?"

Suddenly his eyes widened with realization. "Sorry," he said.

I waited a second. Two seconds. Despite knowing the truth, Noah did not make a move to amend it. The unspoken words seemed to float in the space between us: *I don't think of you in that manner.*

I broke the silence first. "All right. I'll see you tomorrow then. Bye, Noah."

As I walked back to my room, the cold atmosphere made it seem as if I could wave my fingers and a symphony of heartbreaking music would begin playing. He had known after all and hadn't done anything about it. That was enough of an answer for me.

After Miranda's last reaction, I had vowed not to talk about Noah with my girls anymore. However, I needed the support of my best friend, and this time when I spilled everything to her, she was a lot softer.

"I'm sorry."

"Thanks, Miranda."

She scooped a big whop of vanilla ice cream into my bowl. "He's a jerk," she said, and before I could protest, "Guys in general are jerks."

Because it was a female requirement, I clasped my hands together in holy prayer. "Amen."

She petted my hair. "I know. Let's stay in tonight. We can watch sad movies and be dorks and cry together."

I laughed. "You have a boyfriend."

"Your point?"

Later, while both of us were swathed in the warmth of our pillow fort and the scent of half-burned popcorn, I spoke. "You don't think he'll think more about it later and change his mind, do you?" I asked tentatively.

Miranda looked hesitant. There was sympathy that I did not want in her voice. "If I was him, I would wait for the whole situation to blow over. I'd think, 'Maybe if I wait long enough, you'll get over me.'"

She had stated this softly, but I felt it like a kick in my chest anyway. I wilted a little, and then changed the subject, determined to wait until later in my bed, when I could hear only the quiet breathing of my sleeping roommate, to sink full force into loathing.

The answer had been plain in front of my face. Even if Noah was the right guy for me, that didn't mean I was the right girl for him. There had been many signs before, where it was always me making the first leaps forward. I had been blind to the truth because I had been so infatuated with him. He hadn't led me on as much as I had set myself up for disappointment. I couldn't even be angry with him.

The next day I watched from my little empty table in the library as he goofed off with his friends again in their area by the couches. No matter how many times it happened, I didn't think having my interest forgotten by the guy I liked would suck as much as it did. Looking back at most of my heartbreaks, the reactions that I had were more extreme than they needed to be, but knowing this didn't make things any easier.

As an excuse not to do my homework, I pulled out my laptop to check my email. The inbox was loaded with extracurricular letters from my school, but one subject in particular caught my eye. The message was from the University of Illinois Urbana-Champaign: *We've got good news!* I opened the email and scanned through the contents quickly. I had been accepted after all.

It was a small, quiet victory that I couldn't whoop about with my friends. I didn't feel happy enough to jump up in my seat. Still, it felt like I had completed the step of a necessary ritual into adulthood.

I was graduating in three months. Until then and past that point, I had enough time to move on.

ALEXIS
Haley Cao

MAYBE WE MET in another lifetime, and that is why I seem to know your eyes. Maybe you were born in deep valleys, for your voice is firm like the houses of bricks and stones but gentle like the flowing streams of water I am afraid to jump in. Even though I am afraid of drowning, I still dive head first into the crashing tides in hopes that things will work out. Maybe that is my mentality of tackling life, including you.

Maybe we were meant to travel the world, to see the things we always wanted to see. With windows rolled down, I can see myself in the reflection in the side mirror of your car as my hair flips and whips through the edge-cutting air. With one hand on the steering wheel and the other on your own lap, you laugh, echoing through the tunnel, and I am laughing with you. I do not know why we are laughing, but that does not matter.

Maybe my heart will still have palpitations, and my words will still jumble into a mess that no one understands, not even you. But you will laugh it off like you did in the tunnel as your laugh echoes in my memory box of all the things I keep, all the things that matter.

Maybe one day you will stop making me so nervous. I can feel my heart running laps around a track each time you say my name. I can feel my words jumping off a cliff, and I cannot jump after them when I look in your eyes. I can feel my train of thought quickly jumble into a chain that shackles me to the ground, and I am just waiting for another stupid mistake to fall from my mouth. Maybe one day all of that will stop.

I know I talk too much of how your presence intimidates me, and maybe that is not true. Maybe it is the fear of losing you that intimidates me. Maybe it is the knowledge that you are too good for me and that I do not deserve the attention you give me that intimidates me. Perhaps it is the theory that if I say it enough, say that it is you who intimidates me, I will believe that it is not the fear of the unexpected I am trying not to run away from.

Maybe this is what life is supposed to be. A collage of every single squint of your eyes when you smile like the glare of the sun beaming into them. The same eyes I was lost in because I was so sure I had met them before.

All these maybes and possibilities in life are not definite answers to all the outcomes that could, would, and should have happened. Every single possibility is just a strand, and each one is interwoven with the others until they create the single tightrope that I walk across.

No matter how hard I try, I cannot compete with people who have your attention. I cannot give you the things they can because I have nothing to offer but the words on this page. All my life, I have had my words to protect me, and now a single look at you has made them cowards that run away.

For the past year, my life has surrounded around my ability to piece together words until they were phrases, phrases until they were ideas. Yet, you have somehow unraveled these ideas into incoherent words and sounds. I thought my words were invincible, a shield that could protect me from anything harmful, yet you made my shield crumble, and now I am vulnerable.

Alexis, if you do not realize what I am trying to say by now, maybe it is for the best that you never realize at all. Then again, my maybes are strands of a tightrope waiting to snap, and I am just waiting for someone to catch my fall into the crashing tides.

THE SOUL MATE THEORY
Sneh Patel

IN HIGH SCHOOL everything was bigger: class, lockers, the cafeteria, and the all-important hunt for love. At least I thought it was love. But for most of the guys, it was more of a convoluted game of classifying the number of girls they had "gotten with" or of objectifying girls by using the old 1–10 scale. In my first year of high school, I was high on the thrill this addicting game gave me because I wanted to be one of the cool guys. They treated girls like another notch on their belt, throwing them away after they had served their purpose. For me, this game was synonymous with hunting for love.

However, my mind was radically changed when I arrived at the boarding school that I currently attend. My current school is much smaller (and honestly, much smarter) than my previous high school. *Everything* here is different, but I was still addicted to the game, and when I tried to bring my old mentality to my new school, it became clear very quickly that this was not going to work. Girls didn't put up with the crude nonsense that would have gone completely unquestioned at my old school.

What could I do but adapt? I learned to shed my old mentality just like a snake sheds its skin, but now I had no guiding principles to direct my puberty-driven hormones. Wandering around aimlessly, I thought my days with girls were over. Alas, puberty wouldn't have that. I was still physically attracted to girls, and my desire to find someone increased dramatically. I think because I was so blindfolded by this ardent desire to find the perfect girl, I was easily susceptible to falling for someone too hard. And this is exactly what happened. I fell head over heels for a girl in my grade. Her name was Grace, and I thought she could do no wrong.

As the months passed, I obsessed over her more and more. It got to the point where I thought of her when I heard music, I timed when I left my room so I could walk next to her, I did all the stupid things a stupid teenage boy does. All other girls disappeared and I thought she was the only person for me.

Interestingly, this philosophy of one true love has only been around very recently. According to Aziz Ansari's book, *Modern Romance*, up until the 1960s most American relationships were based on security (whether that be financial, social, or personal), and people married after just six months of dating. After multiple interviews with senior citizens, Ansari compiled a list of reasons people got married before the 1960s: "He seemed like a good guy," "she was a nice girl," or "he had a good job."

However, he also conducted a study with a much younger group and their responses to why they were in relationships were astounding. One woman wrote, "He's different from everyone else because: He's a one of a kind human being. There is no one in this world like him. He is stunning, and I am amazed by him every single day. He's made me a better person for having known and loved him. Five years going strong and I'm still obsessed with him. He is my best friend."

Another woman had a similarly beautiful and thoughtful message: "He makes me laugh, and if I don't feel like laughing, he stops and takes the time to find out why. He makes me feel beautiful and loved in my most ugly and unlovable moments. We also share the same faith, work ethic, love of movies and music, and the desire to travel."

This type of love is dubbed "soul mate love" and was very different from the companionate love that dominated the time period before the 1960s. I was one of the many people afflicted by the inane thinking that there was only one person for me, and that person was Grace.

However, even though I had this powerful passion, I was indecisive and timid in her presence. Most of my conversations with her were short and amounted to nothing. She quickly began to view me only as a friend and I seemed to be forever trapped. What had started out as a burning passion, as hot as the forges of Hephaestus, sizzled into nothingness. I was trapped by the idea that she was the only one for me and I could not let her go. I kept telling myself that I needed to push harder because it was destiny for us to be together. Ah, what a simple fool I was, trapped by the same love that had inspired me.

But I got lucky. One night, I had a dream in which I finally mustered up the courage to ask her out. I woke up suddenly and told my roommate, who was still awake. He convinced me to ask her out the following day, something I would never have agreed to do if I had not been drunk on the immediate hubris that the dream had given me. I went back to sleep brimming with confidence. However, when I woke up, I immediately remembered the task at hand and my stomach churned violently, leaving me figuratively and literally floored. I tried to back out of the agreement that I had with my roommate, but he wouldn't hear of it. He called me a few names and told me to "man up." I didn't feel like a man and just wanted to stay in my room the entire day. But I didn't and it was the second greatest decision of my very inchoate love life. (Don't worry, my first greatest decision will be revealed soon.)

After school, I invited Grace over to enjoy the beautiful spring day. I was super nervous and kept trying to phrase my "ask" in different ways in my head. But no matter how much I tried, I couldn't ask her and finally she had to leave. I told myself that it was now or never, so I just did it. Her face became painfully disturbed and she answered with a curt, "No." The moments after were unpleasantly awkward and I responded with "Okay, want to finish ripsticking?" forgetting that she had to leave. Again, her face became painfully disturbed as she said "No, I got to go. Bye."

Most people probably would have become heartbroken over the fact the girl that they loved so passionately had rejected them, but that wasn't the case for me. Strangely, I no longer felt like Atlas burdened by the entire weight of the Earth; I felt free for the first time in a long time. I realized that I didn't love her, or at least I hadn't loved her for the last month. I no longer inserted her name into every love song I heard or stalked her so I could have just a few moments of her time, and I'm an idiot for taking so long to realize it. I was relieved and felt unexpectedly invincible, so I turned around and walked back to my room with some swagger in my step. Over the next few days, I concluded that all this talk about "soul mate love" is absolute garbage. There is no such thing as the one person I am meant for. Honestly, we all just need to find someone to vibe with.

Again, I got lucky because after just a few weeks I found a person I vibe with. She was the girl I went to homecoming with, but I had completely ignored her because of my unfortunate glorification of Grace. Her name was Athena and she epitomized everything about the goddess that she was named after. However, I didn't pursue her like I pursued Grace. I didn't consider Athena to be the only one for me, but I just wanted to talk to her more because we seemed to click. Now, here comes my best decision that I ever made. On April 12, 2015 I asked Athena out after about two weeks of talking to her. I wasn't timid or indecisive when I was with her but rather I was flowing with confidence. Maybe it was because I didn't put any more pressure on the situation than was necessary. She wasn't my soul mate but a really cool girl and that was it. Nothing more, nothing less. The "ask" was pretty romantic, if I were to say so myself. It was raining and I absolutely hate the rain, but she loves it. So, I took her outside and we played in the rain while she laughed and giggled. After we were soaked, I suddenly moved closer to her and looked her directly in the eyes and said, "Do you want to go out with me?" Oh man, her response was so much better than Grace's response. Athena exuberantly said, "Yes!" and she gave me a kiss. Boom! Just like that, we were together. No gazing from afar for months, trying to find the perfect opportunity to strike only to be rejected. This was how it was supposed to be done.

My relationship with Athena grows stronger every day. This type of growth in couples who don't enter relationships with high expectations is supported by the research that Aziz Ansari did. If you compare the incipience of my relationship with an arranged marriage you can see why entering a relationship without the foolish idea of a soul mate can be much more fruitful. Ansari stated that "people in arranged marriages start off lukewarm, but over time they really invest in each other and in general have more successful relationships." People in arranged marriages become steadily happier while the happiness in "soul mate marriages" can rise and fall precipitously, leading to divorces and separations. Now I'm not saying my relationship with Athena was an arranged marriage, but what I am saying is that a relationship is about building something together through communication, honesty, and love. Believing that there is only one person out there for you in a pool of more than seven billion people is just straight dumb. If the "soul mate theory" was correct, then statistically most people would never even meet their one true love.

Anyway my love life is hopefully just beginning, but I have learned some things in my brief run. First, girls are not mere objects that can be measured on an arbitrary scale from 1–10, and the number of girls a guy has hooked up with does not mean anything significant except maybe that he sucks at commitment. Second, soul mates don't exist. I know that sounds harsh, but if you believe there is only one person in the entire world that you match up with, you will never be happy. You will either always be in pursuit of someone who you don't mesh fully with (as I was with Grace) or you'll never be content with a relationship because you will always wonder if there's someone better out there. Last but not least, the chase can be fun, but it is not the end. You have to work diligently to succeed in a relationship. The happiest couples I know are the couples who grow together slow and steady.

INVITATION TO WRITE/*Seven*

WHAT DO YOU THINK *of the idea of a soul mate? Do any of the observations in Sneh Patel's "The Soul Mate Theory" ring true for you? What qualities would your ideal romantic partner possess?*

NEBULOUS LOVE
Gabriella Wallk

I purse my lips in front of the blurry mirror
tinkering with the angle of my chin,
imagining the sweet, soft texture pressing against another's.

In cycles I crave this physical tangibility
to be connected to someone in a palpable fourth dimension
I haven't yet explored.
But the teenage realm consists mainly of hook-ups
and it seems as though people love
to tell the world they loved.

I long for love so real it feels illusionary.
Love that makes the mundane captivating.
Yet questions swirl and I stir
the nagging doubt of sexual orientation without experience,
the omnipresent yet latent fear of asexuality.

If I own myself as a sexual being, where do I set boundaries?
And why must I hide relationships from my parents?
Their romance is in the open, why should mine be shamed?
In the experimental period I creep beneath sheltered, averting eyes,
as my peers set their sights on the upper echelons of sexual experience,
determined to "win" like soccer players seeking trophies.
If I told them I hadn't acquired even a single medal,
what would they say?
This is my warped notion of love.

Yet maybe externalizing my frustrations is
a means of protecting myself from the ache of rejection,
an aversion to the vulnerability and responsibility love forces one to tug on.

How can I be confident and assured
when the untold narrative,
the healthy love,
is hidden within warped notions of consent?

I stand
at the edge of a pier,
awaiting a sign to leap into the intimate, crushing waves,
to swim through the tinted ocean world,
body immersed, soaking, in its spontaneous cool.
Diving into the audacious blues,
I take a risk, stop thinking, let my body be free.
Be confident and whole and happy in who I am
in this strange adventure—"love"—my heart still perceives an illusion.

A DUBIOUS PERCEPTION
Bailey Fox

—————»❤→————

RELATIONSHIPS ARE a trap, and marriage is for people who are too afraid to die alone.

That's what I've grown up believing, what I've grown up being taught, what I've grown up thinking is valid and true.

Children of divorce love differently. Many of us fear love, or maybe the loss of love. We often fear lack of communication but don't know how to communicate. We might not know what a happy, healthy relationship looks like.

Last year I dated another child of divorce. When we started dating, it was awkward, as most first dates are. An interrogation masked by pleasantries occurred during the thirty-minute car ride to the movie theater. I asked about his college experience thus far, "What are you majoring in? What's your favorite class? How do you balance a full-time job with being a full-time student?" as he gripped the steering wheel in his beat-up car, smiling shyly and responding concisely. "I'm not sure yet. Probably computer science. Ha, by not sleeping." In turn, he asked me about my life at home, about the people I hang out with, what I did for fun. I avoided talking about my family, only giving him the bare minimum. I told him about my best friend and explained that my version of fun is hanging out in my friend's basement, playing video games.

At the theater, he introduced me to all the employees we encountered, since he used to work there before transferring to the theater where I work. We watched a children's movie, *Hotel Transylvania 2*. We were in the middle of a row, centered in the theater. Sitting in big, comfy, deep red reclining chairs, we put our feet up and sat in silence.

It was like any movie date. The girl leans closer to the boy, waiting for the boy to make a move. Tension built as I leaned closer, until he finally lifted the armrest between us. His arm wrapped around my shoulder, and I leaned into his warm body.

The movie finished, and I declined going to dinner due to home-work, so he reluctantly drove me home. We had both had fun, so we continued dating.

But then he started texting me more often, good night and good morning texts, while I was at school, while I was with friends. I started to find out more about him, like how his parents got divorced and how he had lived with his grandparents in Ukraine. I didn't tell him about my parents' divorce. He told me about how he lived with his dad, who had been living in America for years, until his dad's girlfriend decided she didn't like him and he got kicked out. I didn't tell him how I switched from my dad's house to my mom's house multiple times a week, or how my dad has kicked me out of his house because he was in a bad mood and I didn't clean my room. He told me how he had been in love with his ex-girlfriend in Ukraine, and how badly she had hurt him. I didn't tell him about my manipulative ex-boyfriend. Instead, I told him I would never hurt him, and he told me that it was going to happen, that I was better than him, that I'd break up with him. I told him he was wrong.

When I found out he'd started calling me his girlfriend after a week, it made me involuntarily cringe. We hadn't talked about being exclusive. I assumed we were just casually dating. He started demanding attention, constantly needing reassurance that I wasn't mad or upset with him, wanting to know stories from my life I wasn't prepared to share. I felt bad; I knew he had almost no friends, so I spent more time with him and texting him. But I'd started losing interest.

Our break-up happened quickly because he gave me a lot of atten-tion, and he needed as much attention in return. I realized quickly that what he needed—attention, affection, love, a meaningful relationship—were things I couldn't give him. I couldn't spend all of my time with him because I had school, homework, and work. He went to night classes at college so he could work during the day. He made the schedule for all the employees at work, and he started giving us the same nights off so we could be together. But I didn't want to spend those nights with someone I began to perceive as needy and clingy. I wanted to hang out with my friends, who were trying to tell me to break up with him because they saw I was unhappy. My friends, who read and analyzed every one of our text conversations and saw how impersonal I had become. My friends, who met him and liked him, yet confirmed my belief that he really wasn't for me. That I needed someone who would text me less, give me space, and who wanted to know more about me without judgment.

During our one month together, I hadn't told him anything personal. He told me everything I ever wanted to know and then some about himself, but I avoided telling him about my life. I avoided telling him about my issues with my dad, my relationship with my mom, my friends, my favorite activities, colors, foods and music. I avoided telling him about anything superficial or deeply personal. I avoided getting close to him. "Relationships are a trap" kept echoing in my mind. My dad's words, "He seems like he's serious. You don't want serious," kept echoing in my mind. My friends' doubtful, "Are you *sure* you like dating him?" kept echoing in my mind.

Just as those ideas have echoed in my mind with every relationship I've had.

As I realized that I didn't want to be in a relationship with him, but also that I didn't want to hurt him, I started having anxiety attacks. Trembling and rocking back and forth, I gasped for air while sitting with my knees to my chest on my bathroom floor. Waves of anxiety crashed over me as I worried about how this would impact our work environment and how he would respond. I didn't know how to break up with him. That week was our one-month anniversary, which I frankly did not care for nor want to celebrate because, congrats, you can tolerate me for one month. That's not much of a feat. There was also Halloween, and I had said I would take him trick-or-treating with my friends and me, since he had never gone before. And his birthday came directly after that; we were planning on going to dinner. I wanted to wait until the week was over so as not to ruin any of these events for him.

But on our one-month anniversary, he sent me a love letter (love text?) that scared me. It was too much, too quickly, and I didn't reciprocate how intensely he felt. I knew that continuing to date him, even for another week, would lead him on, allow him to get more attached, and put me in a negative mental state. I broke up with him not an hour after receiving the text.

My chest felt lighter and I could breathe again.

I grew up in a household where feelings weren't discussed and everything was very factual. When my parents divorced, there was no, "We decided to get a divorce because of reason x, y, and z, and we hope you can understand why this is for the best." It was just, "We're getting a divorce. Here are the rules." When I cried, I was told I shouldn't be crying. I learned, through watching my parents and through our interactions, to hide my feelings. I learned that vulnerability would lead to invalidation, that it's better just to bottle up any emotion.

Had I grown up in a caring environment in which love was looked at in a positive light, maybe the relationship I ended would have been different. Maybe I would have enjoyed the attention and affection. Maybe I would have been more inclined to *try*. Maybe I would have been able to reciprocate the feelings instead of cringing at them.

A part of me is relieved that my perspective of love is so negative that I rarely get hurt. Another, larger part wishes I could have a normal relationship without my fears and experience as a child of divorce getting in the way. This may be how I think for the rest of my life, although I really hope somebody is able to change my dubious perception.

FIRST AND LAST
Eamon Gover

MY FRIENDS TALKED me into going to homecoming last year. I had been very apprehensive about wasting my money like that. All of the money I had was from mowing the lawn or other gigs, but they played the "C'mon dude, quit being a party pooper," card, and I decided to appease them. "Why not?" I thought as I purchased the ticket. It was going to be fun, a guys' night out on the town.

Homecoming night came quickly. We met at a friend's house for photos and our usual shenanigans. My friends had invited a group of girls to go with us, and everybody found a seat in the basement, clustered in our respective cliques. The room had a gentle amber hue, inviting and pleasant. Slowly, our two groups mingled and small talk began, and at first I felt weirded out. However, I put my discomfort aside as I was among friends who encouraged me to take part in the discussion. We all played some foosball, and during one of the games I swore one of the girls was staring at me. Eventually, we left for the dance.

Immediately upon entering the hot and cramped gymnasium, we grabbed a table and I plopped myself down in a chair, pulling out my phone. Before I continue this story, I'd like to say that I hate school dances with a burning passion. I don't understand why people go to them if the only thing that matters is the after-party. Anyway, I was sitting there while my friends had gone off to dance. The music was deafening, and I couldn't think at all. My eyes were aching from the fluorescent lights flashing from all directions. The dance floor was flooded with students. All of a sudden, the girl who had been gazing at me earlier came up to me and asked me to dance. "Sorry, I don't like to dance," I replied hastily. "I prefer to make the music, not dance to it."

Her eyes locked with mine, and somehow that affected me. "Come on, it'll be fun!" she said. I finally caved, and my friends found it hilarious.

Towards the end of the dance, she kissed me. Right on the lips. For a while, too. I'd never felt anything like it, and even now I still recall enjoying it, although I was shocked. I was naive back then—I didn't know how to react. I just stood there, dumbfounded.

Once we all returned to my friend's house for our small and tame after-party, she wouldn't let up. Her dress magnified her curves, and the innocent looks she gave me calmed the unease I expressed outwardly. I couldn't stop anything—it was all beyond the point of comprehension. She asked me to play ping-pong with her. We couldn't find the ball anywhere, but in the process of looking she swooped on me, kissing me passionately. I didn't know what to do; it was really uncomfortable.

"Are you OK?" she asked me with a look of concern.

"Yeah," I whispered back, not wanting to offend her. We went back into the main room, where my friends asked what happened. "I just wanted to play ping-pong," I groaned. They laughed hysterically at that one.

After another hour or two of sitting around doing mostly nothing, I got a ride home from my dad and told him about the situation. I did not know how to proceed. My mind would not work that night. I couldn't figure out why I had been the one she went for. I tried to wrap my mind around it all night long, but came up clueless.

After a refreshing period of silence, she sent me a friend request on Facebook, which I accepted without thinking too hard. We managed to have a pleasant conversation, but soon things went sour.

On a day off of school, she sent me a message. I slept in that day, so I didn't see it until many hours after she sent it. While I was asleep, she thought I was ignoring her. When I finally woke up, she was furious. She started typing insults at me, and I hurled back my own hearty helping of snark. We argued for an hour. She said she regretted "opening up" to me after I had been "manipulating" her. I scoffed out loud, not understanding how a night of making out constituted opening up *or* manipulation. I tried to stay reasonable, but her temper had boiled over. She told me never to talk to her ever again. Honestly, I had no plans of talking to her anyway, so I felt fine, almost happy about ending the fight. Just hours later, however, she tried to apologize, but I said no, since I was extremely irritated at that point. She started ranting about why girls don't like me, but before she could get into detail I unfriended her and blocked her.

I endured so much anxiety from the events of last year's homecoming. I had never felt so uncomfortable and confused before in my life. Call it cliché, call it whatever you like. If only I could go back and change my course of action, I would tell my friends no. No homecoming for me. Not this year. Not any year. No.

A REAL-LIFE FAIRY TALE

Sydney Bakal

CLATTERING HEELS AND panting breaths chase me down the infinite staircase. I can hear his flirtatious pleas as he grips my arm with deliberate grace and spins me around. His fingers curl around my waist, navigating my curves, and caress my neck, tracing hearts on my collarbone. I can feel his smile, cheeks flexing and eyelashes fluttering on my skin. But my heart isn't pounding, and my glands definitely aren't salivating. "Cinderella! Cinderella! Please stay!" he cries, but the clack of my slipper on the pavement is all I hear as I escape.

Cinderella may not be the content of everyone's nightmares, but my dream could have been an excerpt of a John Green book, a Hans Christian Andersen tale, or a description from *The Notebook*. In school, my friends gathered between scenes during musical rehearsals to talk about crushes, steamy make-out sessions, and wet dreams. My cheeks flushed. I was embarrassed not to have experienced any of the above. I began my research and soon stumbled upon a blog about individuals who identified as aromantic and asexual. I hadn't had "sweaty palms" or "a pulsating heart," so I thought I wasn't capable of experiencing romantic love or sexual attraction. Instead of finding comfort with a community of others like me, I was miserable. I stayed up every night till 1:00 a.m. browsing the blog and watching videos, hoping that my lack of feelings would somehow make sense or just go away.

After the final dress rehearsal of our school play, a couple of other cast members gathered around me in the dressing room. One girl behind me announced between giggles, "Julia has the HUGEST crush on you. She talks about you ALL the time, and she is going to ask you out after opening night." I suddenly felt nauseous, nervous, and terrified, so I ran to the bathroom to think in a stall. I silently sobbed for five minutes, then decided I was not going to let this distract me from my real focus, the show. I took one of the abrasive brown paper towels, wiped the racoon mascara from my eyes, and left to look for Julia. I saw her in the theatre lobby surrounded by upperclassmen. "At least turquoise is the best color. It's scientifically proven," she said, mimicking our director's high-pitched voice and overdone hand gestures. Everyone was doubled over laughing. I scooted myself in and grabbed Julia by the arm, pulling her into the next hallway.

She gave me a nervous smile and puppy dog eyes. I took a deep breath and felt like I was going to chuck up the clementines I'd eaten to curb the in-between-show hunger. The muffled voices from the theatre lobby filled the tense silence. I stared up at the white stucco ceiling, and then my eyes drifted back to her anxious face. "It's not that you aren't hilarious, smart, and sweet. I just don't have feelings for people," I some-how choked out. Then I made a run for the back seats of the auditorium to sit in the dark loneliness with my lack of feelings.

Julia was my closest friend, and this wasn't the first time she had feelings for me. Usually, right before our performance of the school's production, she would confess her love. Every time, I would tell her that I didn't have feelings. Why did she keep coming back? Why couldn't I reciprocate her feelings? Was I awful for turning down the one person I cared about? It didn't help that Lauren, my best friend from middle school, had told me, "Come on! Why won't you just give her a chance?! Julia is hilarious, and it's not like you're interested in anyone else." It was true that I didn't like anyone else, and I wasn't sure I ever would. After rehearsal I went home, stared at the ceiling some more, and cried into my pillow, hoping my parents wouldn't hear or ask me any more questions I couldn't answer.

I spent my winter cooped up with my stuffed animals and hot chocolate. School was the same, but I felt lonelier. Julia would come to my locker after school or text me during lunch, but I would go hide in the bathroom or ignore her messages in hopes she would get over her feelings for me and we could just be friends again. At this time, I was getting closer with a girl named Emma who sat at my lunch table. We chatted and talked about her sports, softball and soccer, and I mentioned

I had another show coming up. We exchanged cellphone numbers to give each other more information about our events.

Emma was a bubbly, sports-jersey-wearing tomboy. I went to see a couple of her softball games when the weather improved. The atrocious smell of fresh manure from a nearby stable didn't seem to distract her from making expert catches. We started playing catch during lunch, Emma taking up her usual catcher's stance: squatting low, forearms relaxed on her thighs, with a fierce competition in her eyes. We laughed, ran, and fetched, and when everyone else went inside, we stayed out on the lawn, lying on the grass and staring at the clouds, discussing siblings, parents, and school. Slowly, our conversation turned to relationships. We raved about the novel *I'll Give You the Sun*, in which family relationships are more important than romance. The boring-life-turned-passionate or the make-my-life-not-crap stories seemed too cliché.

A few weeks later, Emma and I were Skyping and she brought up the music video for "Girls Like Girls" by Hayley Kiyoko. It was SOOOO cute. One girl drives her bike to another girl's house. The other girl has a boyfriend, but he seems abusive. The two girls share sideways glances and bond over painting toenails and dancing. In the end, the two girls kiss and the boyfriend discovers them. He begins to yell and slaps his girlfriend, but the other girl beats up the boyfriend, and the two girls kiss while splattered in blood. During the entire video, I longed for someone with whom to share intimate glances, to passionately kiss my blood-spattered face, and to be part of an interesting back-story that would heighten the romance.

During lunch the next day Emma asked if we could go talk. She had dressed up: a little mascara, a dress instead of her usual sports garb, and hair down instead of in a ponytail. We walked up to my locker, making small talk along the way: how did her game go yesterday? What was the score? Were the other girls happy? I thought I knew what she planned to talk about, and I wanted to postpone the discomfort as long as possible. I wasn't ready to lose my new-found best friend.

Finally, we arrived at my locker. Emma leaned against the wall, and then stared up at me, prepared to recite her speech. I looked into my open locker and spent extra seconds pretending to search for missing utensils in my lunchbox. She waited, and then, when I closed my locker, she began. "I really really like you. With you, it's different. I, I wrote you a poem." She took it out and began to recite: "You've been around since middle school, but right around January, I started to see something different. You shined in a new light, and you radiated this… joy." She smiled to herself and then looked up and bit her lip, now nervously awaiting my response.

I looked down, gulped, and then began my practiced response. "You're amazing, Emma. You are so kind, and smart, and talented. I am so flattered. I just don't feel the same way." She looked down at the chevron tiles and her smile disappeared. I wanted her to understand that this was in no way her fault and that I desperately wanted to continue our friendship. "I think I might be asexual and aromantic. I don't have sexual attraction or romantic feelings for anybody. I'm really sorry."

Her forehead wrinkled, and I could tell she was trying to understand. We walked down the stairs back to the cafeteria in heavy silence and sat at opposite ends of the table. She started talking about the Cubs with her friends, and I stared at my computer, pretending to work on an English essay, rewriting the same line again and again and thinking, "What's wrong with me?"

That night, my friend Julia texted me that she thought Emma was flirting with her. All of a sudden my stomach did a little flip, and I felt like I was going to need a bucket. I was lying on the carpet in my bedroom with my chemistry textbook and some galvanic cell diagrams. I swallowed and took some really deep breaths: no puking on chemistry homework. Hadn't Emma just said she liked me? Had she gone so quickly from writing me love poems to flirting with another person? And JULIA! Of all people! My new best friend and my last best friend were going to have the romance I so needed and wanted to feel! I couldn't sleep that night. All I could think about was the "Girls Like Girls" video, but now the girls were Emma and Julia, and I was watching their love story unfold.

The next day, I texted Emma before lunch. *Meet me at my locker? Please?* She showed up with a Bear's jersey and matching blue and orange running shorts, but she wasn't smiling like she had been the day before. The soundtrack to *Pearl Harbor* leaked from the classroom across the hall, and I could hear a toilet flush in the background, quieter than my heavy breaths. I looked into her deep brown eyes and searched for hearts popping out like they did on comic strips. "I'm still figuring out my feelings, but I really care about you, Emma. I want to give this a try." This time I didn't check the chevron tiles for approval.

For the next two weeks, we would Snapchat every night, text all day, and Skype every weekend. We wrote each other love poems and songs. One day after school, the two of us crammed into one of the baby-blue-walled practice rooms. She was plunking out the notes to "Girls Like Girls" on the white, Yamaha piano, while I stood behind her, stroking her sandy-blonde hair. All of a sudden, I felt like I needed to pee, but I knew I didn't have to go to the bathroom. I was entirely caught off guard. We kept talking, and I tried to ignore the sensation, but I thought I knew what it meant. I went home that day and jumped up and down in my room.

After months of worry and confusion, wondering if I could ever be in a relationship or feel attraction, I felt relief. I could be a part of a pair, but in my own way, in my own reality: no glorious, all-consuming, earth-shattering, and immediate passion, but instead a slow building of feelings from months of simple conversation and a couple hours next to a piano. My story isn't Cinderella. The glass slippers make for an interesting metaphor, but Prince Charming saving Cinderella from a life of loneliness and servitude is wish-fulfillment at its peak. I'm satisfied with a reality that isn't a fantasy.

AFTERMATH

Jasmine Cerkleski

WE'VE BEEN BROKEN UP for two years now. I still miss you every now and then. I fell in love with you in seventh grade, and it was hard to know how to handle all of the love we had for each other because no one around us had shown us how. There was only Hollywood to show us what "love" was supposed to be like. We didn't have any real role models for love because my mother left my dad when I was in the fourth grade, and your dad had cheated on your mom when you were younger, and eventually she left him. We didn't know what love was supposed to be.

And love didn't feel the way Hollywood said it would feel. It didn't feel like butterflies all of the time, like happiness every second. I didn't accidentally bump into you in the hallway and then drop my books, only to lock eyes with you and fall in love. Our love story is not some clichéd Hollywood rom-com. You remember how it went, don't you?

You were the new kid in school, bad boy with the eyebrow and lip piercing. You looked different from all the other kids so I couldn't help but stare at you from across the science room. I remember going up to talk to you but you didn't really say much. I had the biggest crush on you for a while, even when you dated that very pretty girl in our class, but you didn't talk to me and I didn't talk to you because I couldn't think of anything good enough to say to you.

Then one day I threw a wet paper ball at you, which I swear was an accident. I meant to throw it at Henry, but he moved and it hit you instead. My face turned bright red and I just whispered an apology from across the lunchroom. I went home and I felt so embarrassed about it, but that same day you messaged me on Facebook. You asked about what happened earlier, and I explained it to you, and even though it was through a message, I was still blushing because in seventh grade, throwing a wet paper ball at your crush by accident is very embarrassing.

After that day we talked and eventually started dating. At first there were butterflies, but when we were in love, those jittery feelings were replaced with so many better things. You showed me what true love feels like, the good and the bad. Love is not just all positive—it hurts. We would sometimes fight for hours because love made us crazy. Do you remember the fights? We fought because of jealousy the most—stupid things like, "Don't talk to him," "Don't hug her," "Don't text him." We were so young and you were all I had. I didn't want anyone to take you from me, but I should've trusted you more and you should've trusted me.

We didn't know how to love or how to express our issues in a mature way because we had no example of this at home. My father was always yelling for no reason and your family was always arguing over petty things. We developed our families' bad habits, but even so, we always came back to each other with love at the end of the day. You taught me forgiveness, trust, and so many other things. I learned so much from you and I hope you can say the same.

Our lives were far from perfect. Our families were crazy, school sucked, friends were fake, but when I was with you none of that mattered. Everything was perfect when it was just you and me. And that's what I really don't understand about love. How can you love someone so much that when you're with them all of your troubles go away, and then one day just not feel that way anymore? How does love just fade away?

Love is confusing. We loved each other so much until our ninth grade year was over, or at least that's when I noticed a change. Freshman year of high school I started doing your homework because you didn't want to, and I didn't want to see you fail. By the end of freshman year I was tired of doing your homework. I was becoming independent, and you just kept depending on me. I was maturing but you stayed the same. I always thought we would grow together, but instead I grew out of you.

In the beginning of sophomore year, you began to fail your classes because I wasn't doing your homework, and then you started missing days because I stopped calling you every morning to wake you up. You were failing and you didn't care. And I was tired of caring for the both of us. Love was replaced with pent-up anger. Over time, I became angry and disappointed in who you were becoming. I didn't feel like your girlfriend anymore, I felt like I was becoming your mother because you were acting like a little boy.

When we broke up you dropped out, and I didn't hear from you until three months later. We met up to catch up on everything and you had not changed a bit, but I felt like I had changed so much. You told me you were attending an alternative school and a few months later you dropped out of there, too. That was almost a year ago. That was the last I heard from you. I wonder how you're doing now. I wonder so many things about you. I never wanted for us to become strangers, and I still care for you and your family deeply. I love who you were and I hope one day someone will love who you have become.

DO YOU EVER FEEL CONFLICTED *because of what's expected of you in relationships? Where does the expectation come from—cultural models, parents and families, friends, yourself? How have you responded to the conflict?*

WRITING FROM IMAGES

INSPIRATION FOR WRITING *can come from anywhere —
experience, an overheard conversation, music, a play or film, works of art.
The following images, created by Chicagoland teens in classes at Marwen,
all depict or comment on the idea of relationships in some way.*

CHOOSE ONE *of these images, or the whole group together, as a jumping-off point, and start to write. Don't plan out what you're going to say, just see where the images lead you.*

Angelina Schrode

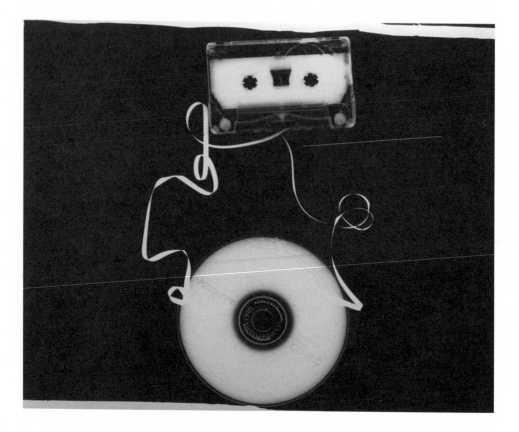

Cleo Clark

Irene Lu

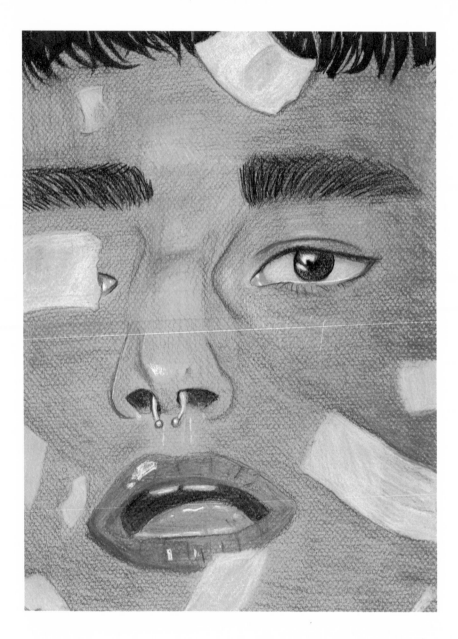

My Tam Vo

Faviola Anaya Esquivel

Billie Murray

Davita Miranda

Sophia Clason

Nurrah Muhammad

Anny Solano

Anna Korol

Gabriela Larios

MORE INVITATIONS TO WRITE

HERE ARE SOME MORE *writing prompts to jump-start your creativity.
Our advice: choose one, turn the page (or use a separate notebook or computer
screen) and set a timer. Give yourself 5 or 10 minutes, no distractions,
and write as quickly as possible. You might be surprised by what comes out!*

1. What do you wish your parents, teachers, and any
   other adults in your life understood about the way teens
   experience relationships?

2. What does a healthy relationship look like to you? Where
   have you witnessed this?

3. Write a portrait of someone you've loved. Use specific
   details to capture the person's character, including gestures,
   mannerisms, ways of speaking, impulses. Without telling
   readers outright what appealed to you about this person,
   show your attraction.

4. Write a poem or piece of prose in list form. (See Izzy
   Dimiceli's "Don't" for inspiration.)

5. Who was the first person — real, imaginary, even celebrity —
   you had a crush on? Write about what you remember thinking
   and feeling.

6. Consider the pressure some teens feel to label their sexuality. Is that something you've experienced or witnessed? What challenges and/or opportunities do you see presented by labels?

7. Taking inspiration from the structure of Georgia Cienkus's "Forgettable," write about a single experience that you interrupt with a flashback to a different experience.

8. What's your favorite depiction of a relationship in a book, movie, TV show, or song? Why?

9. Write about a hard lesson you've learned from a relationship— your own or someone else's.

10. Write from a question. Your own, someone else's, perhaps a question you've often heard repeated. Think about not just an answer but why the question is important.

11. Write from exaggeration. Take a good or bad trait (your own or someone else's) and blow it all out of proportion. See what this caricature ultimately leads you to, idea-wise.

12. Write a set of guidelines for teens trying to navigate their first (or second or third...) romantic relationship.

ACKNOWLEDGMENTS

THIS BOOK, like all the Big Shoulders Books volumes, would not be possible without the generous support and continued inspiration of Bill and Irene Beck.

Thanks to graduate and undergraduate students in the DePaul English Department's Book Editing and Book Promotion courses: Elizabeth Bradley, Michelle Donfrio, Kat Ellinger, Chandler Garland, Amanda Graber, Eric Houghton, Audrey Juergens, Kaitlyn Kesler, Katherine LaTour, Kaitlyn Lounsberry, Rosie McCarty, Jim McDoniel, Moriah Meeks, Gabriella Mihm, Zoe Nepolello, Laura Niebrugge, Kathrine Popielarz. Ethan Safron, Brittany Schmitt, Samantha Schorsch, Jasmina Selimovic, Anne Terashima, Drew Weissman.

Of these students, we would like to acknowledge the exceptional efforts of Eric Houghton, Audrey Juergens, and Drew Weissman, all of whom went above and beyond to cultivate submissions. In addition, Eric Houghton, Drew Weissman, Rosie McCarty, and Kaitlyn Kessler contributed much-appreciated editing even after their course had ended. We would also like to thank Dana Kaye for her expertise and energy in teaching the book promotion course.

Big Shoulders Books has been a labor of love since Chris Green, Miles Harvey, and Michele Morano founded it in 2012. Many thanks to Chris and Miles, as well as to Managing Editor Dave Welch and graduate assistant and copyeditor, Eric Houghton. We are grateful for support provided by the DePaul University Departments of English and Women's and Gender Studies, the College of Liberal Arts and Social Sciences, and the Beck Research Initiative for Women, Gender, and Community. Natalie Bontumasi contributed not only her extraordinary talent as a book designer but also a generous, collaborative spirit that we greatly appreciate.

The following Chicagoland schools are represented in this book: Alcott College Prep, Amundsen High School, Barrington High School, Carl Schurz High School, Chicago High School for the Arts, CICS Northtown Academy, Curie Metropolitan High School, Homewood-Flossmoor High School, Horizon Science Academy, Illinois Mathematics and Science Academy, Lakeview High School, Larkin High School, Lincoln Park High School, New Trier High School, Prosser Career Academy, Walter Payton College Preparatory High School, Whitney M. Young Magnet High School, and Winston Campus Junior High School.

We are very grateful to the educators, librarians, and community members who helped connect us with teen contributors and to the many teachers who supported this project in their classrooms, including Ariell Bachmann, Tina Boyer Brown, Ed Ernst, Julie Kurowaski-Jaquez, Billy Lombardo, Sahar Mustafah, Cecelia Pinto, Stephanie Rittner, Kenyatta Rogers, Jasmina Selimovic, and Dr. Karen Torme-Olson. Thanks to Moki Tantoco of the National Veterans Art Museum in Chicago for sharing our prompts with her teen writing group and to Julie Koslowsky and Jennifer Steele of the Chicago Public Library for connecting us with all the attendees of the 2016 ChiTeen Lit Festival. We would also like to acknowledge the extraordinary work of Marwen, which provides free studio art courses to Chicago students in under-resourced communities and schools, some of whom contributed images to this anthology. Thank you to Cynthia Weiss for facilitating their participation.

Above all, thank you to the young people who shared their work, and to those inspired by that work to record their own experiences within these pages.

ABOUT THE EDITORIAL TEAM

BETH CATLETT (Co-Editor) is Associate Professor and Chair of the Department of Women's and Gender Studies at DePaul University. She is the co-founder and Director of the Beck Research Initiative for Women, Gender, and Community that specializes in community-based research involving gendered violence and social movements to create community change. Her areas of scholarly interest include youth leadership and activism, community-based participatory action research, violence in intimate relationships, and the uses of contemplative practices to inspire social justice.

MICHELLE FALKOFF (Foreword) is the author of *Playlist For The Dead* (2015), *Pushing Perfect* (2016), and *Questions I Want To Ask You* (2018). She studied literature at the University of Pennsylvania, law at Columbia Law School, and creative writing at the Iowa Writers' Workshop. She lives and teaches in Chicago, where she directs the first-year legal writing program at Northwestern Pritzker School of Law and occasionally teaches creative writing at the University of Chicago and elsewhere.

CHRIS GREEN (BSB Founding Editor) is the author of *The Sky Over Walgreens*, *Epiphany School*, and *Résumé*. His poetry has appeared in such publications as *Poetry*, *The New York Times*, *New Letters*, and *Nimrod*. He has edited four anthologies, including *I Remember: Chicago Veterans of War*. He teaches in the English Department at DePaul University. More information can be found at www.chrisgreenpoetry.com.

MILES HARVEY (BSB Founding Editor) is the editor of *How Long Will I Cry?: Voices of Youth Violence*, a collection of oral histories now in its sixth edition with more than 38,000 copies in circulation. His other books include *The Island of Lost Maps: A True Story of Cartographic Crime*. He is an associate professor of English at DePaul University.

NATALIE MILLS BONTUMASI (Book Designer) is the owner and principal designer of Good Thomas Design. She is especially passionate about working for non-profit organizations, and recently designed *I Remember: Chicago Veterans of War* for Big Shoulders Books. Her work is included in the Chicago Design Archive.

MICHELE MORANO (Co-Editor and BSB Founding Editor) is the author of *Grammar Lessons: Translating a Life in Spain* and many published essays and stories. She is Associate Professor and Chair of the English Department at DePaul University.

DAVE WELCH (BSB Production Manager) is the author of *It Is Such a Good Thing to Be in Love with You* (GreenTower Press) and has published poems in journals including *Boston Review*, *Colorado Review*, and *Kenyon Review Online*. The recipient of awards from the Academy of American Poets, The Poetry Society of America, and The Sewanee Writers Conference, he is Assistant Director of Literacy Programs and Outreach in the English Department and the Center for Latino Research at DePaul University, and he serves on the Associate Board of 826CHI.

GET INVOLVED:

Community Organizations for Teen Writing

THE FOLLOWING NONPROFIT organizations offer programming to Chicago teens interested in working on their writing. This is by no means an exhaustive list. These organizations are also in need of volunteers, donations, and support.

826CHI
826chi.org
Dedicated to supporting students aged 6 to 18 with their creative and expository writing skills, and to helping teachers inspire their students to write. 826Chi regularly publishes the work of young Chicago writers.

AFTER SCHOOL MATTERS
afterschoolmatters.org
Provides life-changing after-school and summer program opportunities to more than 15,000 Chicago high school teens each year.

CHITEEN LIT FEST
chiteenlitfest.org
An annual event that creates a safe and creative space for young adults to unlock and discover their unique voice through literary arts. Seeks to bring together young people from across Chicago and celebrate their talents as they express themselves through exceptional and honest art.

CHICAGO LITERACY ALLIANCE
chicagoliteracyalliance.org
Formed with a collective passion to help people of all ages and backgrounds receive the critical literacy support they need, from basic education and tutoring through enrichment, literary arts, and book distribution.

COMMUNITY TV NETWORK

ctvnetwork.org

Empowers low-income young adults and children in Chicago by engaging them in the creative and collaborative process of digital video production.

DO THE WRITE THING NETWORK

dothewritethingchicago.org

Gives middle school students an opportunity to examine the impact of violence on their lives in classroom discussions and in written form by communicating what they have seen to be the causes of youth violence as well as solutions to help decrease the violence in their communities.

LOUDER THAN A BOMB

youngchicagoauthors.org/louder-than-a-bomb

An annual event hosting over 1,000 youth poets for a month of Olympic-style poetry bouts, workshops, and special events. Students representing schools and community groups in the Chicago area perform original solo and group poems in a tournament-style competition.

OPEN BOOKS

open-books.org

Provides literacy experiences for tens of thousands of readers each year through inspiring programs and the creative capitalization of books.

POETRY CENTER OF CHICAGO—HANDS ON STANZAS PROGRAM

poetrycenter.org/hands-on-stanzas

A creative literacy residency program in Chicago Public Schools in which poets-in-residence meet with classes weekly and publish student work after each session on the Hands on Stanzas school blogs. The program improves reading and writing skills, builds confidence, and affirms the voices of young Chicagoans.

POLYPHONY H.S.

polyphonyhs.com

An international student-run literary magazine for high school writers.

SHE CREW

shecrew.org

Gives girls twelve to fourteen the opportunity to express themselves, have their voices heard, and make new friends in a safe and female positive environment.

STREET-LEVEL YOUTH MEDIA

street-level.org

Educates Chicago's urban youth in media arts and emerging technologies for use in self-expression, communication, and social change.

STORYCATCHERS THEATRE

storycatcherstheatre.org

Prepares young people to make thoughtful life choices through the process of writing, producing, and performing original musical theatre inspired by personal stories.

THE WRITERS AND ARTISTS PROJECT

twaap.org

Mentors teenagers in the arts — including writing, spoken word, theater, visual arts, and music — in order to facilitate their self-expression and self-empowerment.

YOUNG CHICAGO AUTHORS

youngchicagoauthors.org

Exposes young people to hip-hop realist portraiture and teaches them how to create their own authentic narratives through a variety of arts education programs both in and out of the classroom.